The Growth Director's Secret

Why businesses struggle to grow – and
what you can do to change it

Andrew Brent

Bloomsbury Business
An imprint of Bloomsbury Publishing Plc

B L O O M S B U R Y
LONDON · OXFORD · NEW YORK · NEW DELHI · SYDNEY

Bloomsbury Business

An imprint of Bloomsbury Publishing Plc

50 Bedford Square	1385 Broadway
London	New York
WC1B 3DP	NY 10018
UK	USA

www.bloomsbury.com

BLOOMSBURY and the Diana logo are trademarks of Bloomsbury Publishing Plc

First published 2017

© Andrew Brent, 2017

British Library Cataloguing-in-Publication Data
A catalogue record for this book is available from the British Library.

ISBN:	HB:	978-1-4729-3629-5
	ePDF:	978-1-4729-3630-1
	ePub:	978-1-4729-3631-8

Library of Congress Cataloging-in-Publication Data
A catalog record for this book is available from the Library of Congress.

Cover design by Liron Gilenberg
Cover image © xubingruo/iStock

Typeset by RefineCatch Limited, Bungay, Suffolk
Printed and bound in Great Britain

Table of Contents

Preface

If you work for a business – any business – here's a simple question:

What's the name of your Growth Director?

What? You don't have a 'Growth Director'?

Why not? You have a Finance Director, don't you? And a Marketing Director? Probably a Sales Director too – or, if you're a retailer, then a Stores Director. You're sure to have an HR Director, almost certainly an IT Director and probably a Legal Director as well – even if this role doesn't sit on your Exco.

Those of you in big, funky, complex organisations might well have a New Product Development Director, quite likely a PR Director (although they may report to the Marketing Director) and possibly even a Sustainability Director.

I've even heard some companies have a Director of First Impressions (it turned out this was a neat – and appropriate – title for the Receptionist!).

But no Growth Director – really?

If you haven't got a Growth Director, who's responsible (and accountable) for growth in your company? Who brings the growth strategy to the Exco and reports progress against it? Who is rewarded when you're growing strongly? More pertinently, who is fired when growth goes backwards?

If you couldn't answer these questions very easily, then don't worry – you're not alone.

Incredibly, of the 50 leading listed consumer companies in the US and the UK where data was available, just one (Mondelez) had a Growth Director position on their Excos. Compare that with the other key executive positions:

Executive positions	Finance director	Marketing director	IT director	HR director	Legal director	Growth director
Percentage of companies with these roles (sample of 50 leading UK and US companies)	100%	58%	53%	86%	77%	2%

So who **is** responsible for growth in consumer companies?

Our interactions with many leading consumer companies have found that there is no clear answer to this. The most common response is 'the whole Executive team'; effectively, this means no-one assumes lead responsibility. Some CEOs would claim they 'own' growth – but do they really have the time (or the skills) to focus on this in the right way? Quite often we will find two or three different executives saying 'I do'. That lack of clarity and the potential for role conflict is a recipe for confusion.

Does this even matter? Well, we think it does. We believe that if no individual feels personally responsible for growth (and is accepted by their colleagues as having this lead responsibility), then it is most likely that the business will lose focus against this key area.

After all, how confident would you feel in your company delivering its bottom line numbers if there was no Finance Director to hold the team to account? How likely is it that your IT systems would work effectively without an IT Director to pull them together? Would your teams implement consistent policies on remuneration, training or recruitment without an HR Director to set standards and monitor implementation? Who would get the blame for the advertising not working if there was no Marketing Director to assume responsibility?

Yet such a lack of accountability is commonplace when it comes to growth.

This book presents much evidence that growth is just about the least-well-managed area of most companies' operations. Very few companies deliver significant, sustained growth year after year – and this has become almost accepted, as long as they deliver their bottom line profit targets.

We believe that one fundamental reason for this chronic under-performance is the clear lack of accountability for growth in almost all major corporate environments. Growth has almost become 'the thing that happens when everything else goes well'.

We believe this is not good enough.

We believe this lack of accountability for growth leads to a lack of focus at Exco level about what it takes to grow significantly, sustainably and profitably. This lack of focus leads, in turn, to a lack of understanding of how growth 'works' and allows companies to make some basic mistakes in developing and implementing their commercial strategies.

Most fundamentally, the lack of accountability for growth means that most companies do not have a recognised growth strategy (profit plans – yes; revenue targets – yes; sales plans – yes; growth strategy – no) identifying clearly which customers will be targeted as the primary sources of growth, what propositions will be presented to them to secure incremental sales, how these will be delivered, and how marketing plans will effectively target the highest-potential customers.

Without the clarity of a growth strategy to direct corporate efforts and focus deployment of resources, you can be sure many companies are underperforming in this key business area. In fact, we say that even if you do not have a 'Growth Director' position on your Exco, you need to think and act as if you do.

So how would a Growth Director help your business to deliver transformational growth?

Well, they might help by showing you:

- How to map the markets in which you operate to identify the areas which provide the biggest growth opportunities for your business (there may be fewer than you think).
- How to identify the core group of 'Market-Making' Customers who should be your key targets and who, once 'sold' on your brands, will become incredibly powerful and commercially effective advocates for your business.

- How new findings from the field of neuroscientific behavioural economics are revealing how consumers are hard-wired to shop in certain ways and how, once companies understand this, they can begin to orientate their propositions to ensure their brands are chosen more frequently.
- How to identify the key 'Brand Choice Moments' that determine long-term brand preference in every business category – and how the companies that 'own' these moments are delivering growth, year after year.
- Why your company must learn to focus its teams on developing propositions, products and services that are significantly preferred at these key Brand Choice Moments, and how to do this.
- How you need to be prepared to reinvent traditional approaches to marketing to focus relentlessly against building advocacy with 'Market-Making' customers at these key moments and step-changing marketing spending efficiency via a new approach of 'Marketing at Open Minds'.

In the absence of a genuine Growth Director, this book will show you how to do all of these things.

As you move through the chapters you will, from time to time, encounter our fictitious Growth Director – asking questions, relating anecdotes, and summarising insights. While these may not be entirely real, our Growth Director represents an amalgam of the knowledge and experience acquired by the author and key contributors to this book over careers spent at the top of major consumer businesses in the UK, Europe, the US, Asia and the rest of the world.

Our intention is that our Growth Director will reveal much of what you need to know if you are to significantly improve your company's chances of embedding the practices of significant, sustained and profitable growth.

So we suggest you listen to them carefully.

You never know – you might just discover The Growth Director's Secret . . .

Chapter 1

The Growth Paradox: Why growth is so important – and why so few businesses are good at delivering it

Growth is, by some distance, the single most valuable attribute that a business can have. Businesses that grow significantly year after year deliver higher margins, lower costs and much stronger profit growth than equivalently sized companies who are not growing at the same rate.

Growing companies receive disproportionate support from retailers and distributors, have more highly energised and motivated workforces, and are preferred places for talented people to work.

Perhaps most importantly for many CEOs, we live in a commercial world where financial markets focus more on corporate growth prospects than any other financial measure. Put simply, sustained and significant growth is the single biggest determinant of share price appreciation and shareholder returns.

In short – growth rocks! Or, at least, some growth does.

Growth of any type simply requires more consumer purchases of your products and services – either through more people buying or through the same number of people buying more frequently or in larger quantities. There are two ways of generating these additional purchases – but only one of them is worth having.

Option 1: 'Buy' more consumer purchases

This pattern of behaviour is easily recognised:

- an over-reliance on promotions;
- frequent price-cutting;

- disproportionate retailer/distributor investment to 'buy' listings/space/promotional support;
- 'initiative-itis' that pushes lots of new ideas (often short-term/unsuccessfully) into the market to generate short-term sales uplifts; and
- even growth via cycles of acquisition.

We call this 'false growth'. This may boost the top-line, but tends to be very expensive, often downright unprofitable, organisationally complex (often introducing hard-to-identify hidden 'costs of complexity'), temporary in its impact (your promotional sales spike will be offset by your competitor's reaction next month) and is highly unlikely to generate growth that is sustainable, significant or, most importantly, profitable.

If you've spent any time working in large consumer-focused organisations, you will almost certainly recognise these characteristics – way too many companies are lulled into chasing such 'false growth'.

Option 2: 'Recruit' more consumer purchases

Recruitment is much harder to achieve, but is much more valuable.

Recruiting consumers means attracting consumers to you because they understand your proposition, feel it is more relevant to their needs and prefer it to those of other businesses. Recruited consumers do not need constant promotions to maintain their purchasing. While they won't ever turn down a price cut, they are happy to buy at full price. Their loyalty influences retailers and distributors to list/support your brands. Their advocacy will market your brand to others – for free! Their genuine commitment to the proposition offered by your brand means that the growth they generate is more likely to be sustainable, significant and profitable.

We call this 'Good Growth' and it is the only type of growth worth having. It can only be achieved by offering to consumers a proposition sufficiently attractive that more and more of them will want to buy it, month after month and year after year. Good Growth results in:

- growth driven by increasing penetration of your market;
- existing users becoming more loyal and buying more frequently;
- users happy to buy at full price – reduced reliance on price/ promotional spend;
- users who are active advocates for your brand; and
- growth that is likely to drive top line and margin up, costs down and, of course, bottom line profit strongly upwards.

For the rest of this book, whenever we refer to growth, we mean Good Growth.

So, to go back to where we started: Good Growth rocks! But don't take our word for it. Many of the world's smartest business thinkers have already reached the same conclusion:

> 'Outperformance in revenue growth is correlated with the superior creation of shareholder value.'
>
> *McKinsey Quarterly 2008; survey of 200 global companies*

> 'Top-line growth is vital for corporate survival. Companies whose revenue increased more slowly than GDP were five times more likely to succumb (to acquisition).'
>
> *McKinsey Quarterly May 2007; survey of 100 top US companies*

> 'Investors are giving management less time than ever ... they ... demand not merely growth, but growth each and every quarter.'
>
> Zook (2001)

Or, as McKinsey and Co puts it with glorious simplicity:

> 'In a challenging environment, growth matters more than ever. Growth is magic!'
>
> *Yuval Atsmon and Sven Smit, McKinsey Quarterly October 2015*

Take a look at the statistics from a survey of over 600 companies carried out in 1972 by the *Harvard Business Review* (Figure 1.1 and 1.2), which illustrate how strong the correlation was between growth (measured in this case by growth in market share) and profitability.

The data seems incredibly clear – and (unusually) most successful business leaders all seem to be completely in tune. Delivering significant, sustained growth is the most valuable achievement that a management team can deliver.

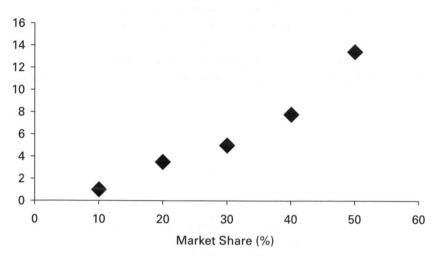

Figure 1.1 'As market share rises . . . profit margin on sales increases sharply' Buzzell et al. (1975)

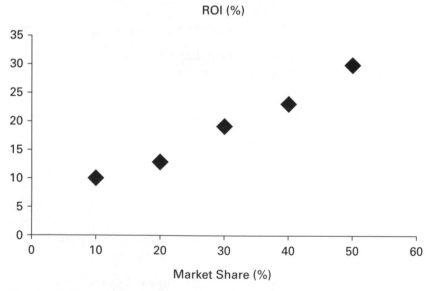

Figure 1.2 'There is no doubt that market share and ROI are strongly related. On average, a difference of 10% points in market share delivers a difference of 5 percentage points in pre-tax ROI' 'Buzzell et al. (1975)

Yet, despite its disproportionate impact on corporate results, growth is routinely the least well-managed part of most major companies' operations. While executive responsibility for profit, people, sales, the supply chain, information technology (IT), brand building, research and development (R&D) and legal are almost always assigned to one individual on the executive team, responsibility for delivering growth is rarely the responsibility of any single individual.

Many executive committees (Excos) would claim 'we all share ownership for our growth'. Unfortunately, this means that no-one really owns it. Some chief executives would claim that they 'own' growth. However, a fully functioning chief executive officer (CEO) does not have the time, or more typically the skill-set, to execute this responsibility effectively. Some organisations might claim that either the marketing director or the sales director 'owns' growth; however, this is rarely accompanied by the authority necessary beyond the traditional remit of advertising and promotions/retailer relationships to deliver a genuine strategic growth plan. Of greater concern, given the crucial importance of this key corporate performance metric – if no-one around the Exco table feels accountable to their colleagues for delivering growth then the chances are that it won't happen.

Partly as a result of this lack of accountability, while almost every company could quickly provide details of its plans for cost-savings, margin improvement, product initiatives, training and development, and sales and marketing (each with admirable clarity on objectives and goals, key strategies, what needs to be done by when, and who owns each identified deliverable), very few companies could produce a similarly concise and actionable plan for growth with clarity on which consumers are providing new business, how those consumers will be persuaded to switch, and what needs to be done to propositions/products/marketing plans to ensure the delivery of the growth objectives outlined.

The modern corporate mindset seems often to be 'growth is what happens when you get all the other areas of your operation right'. In our opinion, this view is superficial, complacent, and just plain wrong.

This leads to what we call the Growth Paradox – *significant, sustained growth is undoubtedly the most valuable asset a business can have …*

and yet growth is routinely the least well-managed aspect of a company's business.

Almost all businesses regard consistent growth as one of their most important strategic deliverables, yet most businesses lack clear accountability for growth at Exco level, fail to develop anything resembling a clear strategic growth plan, and accept a culture of compensating for annual under-performance versus growth targets via cost savings/margin improvements/price rises. That's a huge, and troubling, paradox.

Think we're exaggerating? Think again:

> Since 2000, 90% (of the companies in our surveys) have failed to hit the growth projections in their annual reports.
>
> Allen (2014)

> Given investor expectations of quarter-by-quarter growth, 99 out of 100 management teams will fail to meet investor expectations.
>
> Zook (2001)

What causes this damaging and puzzling paradox? Well, in a word, we think it's *Stuff*.

If you've ever worked in business, you'll be familiar with the 'Stuff' we mean:

- pressure to hit the week's/month's/quarter's sales targets;
- sudden unwelcome movements in market share (... 'Don't panic!' ...);
- unexpected competitive activity ... or, worse still, new competitive product initiatives;
- pressure from retailers/distributors;
- technology changes (gotta keep up ...);
- smart new ideas; (sometimes from the chairman's golf buddy);
- hot new advertising campaigns;
- apparent failure of the last Hot New Advertising Campaign;
- 'helpful' feedback from the board meeting.

All of these things, and many more, place additional pressure on the Exco team to 'do stuff – quickly!' in order to deliver on the company's short-term sales and profit goals. This is usually done at speed, with little help from consumer data to guide decision making, under short-term cost pressures and with success measured by irredeemably short-term metrics such as monthly sales results or bi-monthly market shares.

These inevitable market/organisational pressures, and the complexity they bring, cause businesses to lose sight of the fundamentals that determine whether or not they are positioned to grow. In a continuous search for the 'magic' commercial proposition or marketing plan that will stave off those short-term sales/profit pressures, they become locked into an expensive and ineffective cycle of proliferating initiatives, 'always on' sales/promotional plans, constantly changing 'butterfly' marketing campaigns and an over-reliance on price cutting or promotions to stimulate flagging sales.

Typically, this leads to larger and more expensive organisational structures, bland and undifferentiated commercial propositions, and costly and ineffective sales and marketing programmes. Sound familiar?

No-one should be blamed for this . . . it's just how businesses work.

It's not just us who have noticed how this '*Stuff*-driven complexity' slows even the best businesses down:

> An organisation becomes bewildered rather than energised when it is asked to do too much at once.
>
> Hammer and Champy (1993)

> What kills future growth is not the market, but your own internal complexity . . . (and) complexity is the silent killer of growth.
>
> Allen (2014)

> During turbulent times . . . it is the choice and depth of focus . . . that leads to sustained, profitable growth.
>
> Zook (2001)

It's clear that businesses need to become better – much better – at driving sustained, significant growth. It's also clear that, in order to do this, they need to find ways to break through the storm of *Stuff* that drives complexity and cost and distracts them from the crucial task of developing simple, powerful plans that their organisations can focus on to maximise the growth potential of their businesses.

It is, however, possible to break out of this damaging cycle. Possible – though not necessarily easy.

I asked the Growth Director for advice on how to go about doing this. Here's the advice I received:

Exco responsibility (and accountability) for growth MUST be clear and must sit with one individual

In the Growth Director's opinion, unless one member of the Exec team feels the hot breath of the CEO on his/her shoulder when growth is not being delivered, then it is most unlikely that the subject will ever get the attention, focus and resource allocation it needs.

Our view remains that appointing a Growth Director is the best way to do this – but if this feels a bit too radical, then you need to officially designate one Exco member with 'Growth Director' responsibilities – and then hold them to account.

Growth needs to be an important Exco priority – your agendas will tell you whether it is or not

Way too many Exco teams pay lip-service to growth as a strategic objective. If an Exco is not discussing growth regularly, is not devoting people and financial resources to developing/implementing growth plans, and is not ensuring that each department is supporting the growth agenda, then we would say it is not taking the subject seriously.

A useful benchmark is to compare the number of times growth is an agenda item at Exco/board meetings compared with, say, cost savings, people/organisational development issues or new product development. By 'growth discussion' we do not mean 'reviewing business performance/

results' – we mean 'discussing where future growth will come from and how well set up we are to achieve it'. If growth does not receive a significant share of Exco attention, don't be surprised if your company fails to deliver it.

There MUST be a clear, simple, growth strategy with which all Exco members are familiar

That means it must be written down – ideally on just one or two pages. Just in the same way that they'll recognise the budget plan, the cost-saving plans, the new product launch timetable, and the annual performance review plan, your Exco need to be able to articulate the outline of your growth strategy – prioritised sources of growth, agreed growth proposition, resources to be allocated to deliver growth, growth goals and targeted delivery timings.

If they can't do this (and many can't), then the chances are you do not have an organisation which is aligned behind a plan to deliver growth –so you'll probably fail to grow.

You need a set of growth goals that go beyond your three-year budget plans

Budgets are set to be delivered, are usually reasonably conservative, and are typically based on an implicit assumption that the business will continue to run as it has done over the past few years – but a little bit better.

To be meaningful and to drive the type of focused behaviour that organisations need to demonstrate to cut through all the '*Stuff*' and deliver real growth, growth goals should aim to grow significantly beyond an organisation's budgeted targets. This will, in itself, force healthy questions and discussions, such as:

• Where will our growth come from?

- Do we need to change/enhance our proposition to deliver this?
- What is the cost of these changes and will they pay out?
- How effective are our marketing programmes at targeting our highest-growth customers and how should we change them to grow faster?

If you're not having discussions like these, you're probably not stretching far enough to deliver real growth. Go back and challenge your growth goals.

Your Growth Director needs to be empowered to deliver the growth strategy

That means ensuring alignment across the Exco (and therefore across the whole organisation) behind the growth strategy, as well as behind the changes to proposition/targeting/marketing and sales plans that it is likely to imply.

When an Exco agrees a challenging cost-saving target, the CFO will feel empowered to extract savings from all parts of the business; an Exco that is genuinely committed to growth will empower their Growth Director to receive the support he/she needs from across the business. This must also mean people, time and budgets being made available to deliver the growth strategy – and a shared commitment across the Exco to find these as and when they are needed.

Nothing kills growth strategies more than a 'lip service' agreement from Exco teams followed by a refusal to provide resources/support when these are required.

Consumer/customer data needs to be of the very best quality

Ultimately, successful growth strategies are built on real clarity about which consumers/customers represent the best growth prospects, what it will take to persuade them to choose your brands, and how best to communicate efficiently and persuasively with them. Does your company have a deep enough understanding of its customers to make these choices with confidence? If not, do whatever it takes to reach this understanding.

Remember – all sales, and therefore all growth (and, of course, all profit), come ultimately from your customers. You cannot expect to grow effectively if you do not understand what they want. Your growth strategy will certainly fail if the consumer/customer data from which it is derived is not good enough.

You need to embed effective growth metrics to understand and monitor progress

Simple revenue growth is not a good growth metric on its own. Revenue growth can be generated in many different ways, but many of these do not lead to sustainable, profitable growth – refer back to the section above on 'false growth'.

Market share is a better metric than revenue alone, but even this is still prone to short-term promotionally driven fluctuations that make it unreliable as an indicator of good growth.

You will need to agree appropriate metrics to measure the progress of your growth strategy and report on these regularly. Metrics are likely to differ according to the nature of each business, but would typically include some measure of share of purchases amongst target consumers/ customers, which is linked, in turn, to metrics measuring strength of satisfaction/propensity to be advocates amongst those key consumer/ customer groups.

Whatever measure is right for your business, ensure it is embedded properly; use it as the key indicator of the success of your growth strategy. If you get these metrics right, they will help 'stiffen the Exco spine' through times when revenues can fluctuate worryingly. Keeping the strategy on track is not easy; top-quality metrics will help you to make the right decisions.

Review progress regularly. If you're not talking about growth, then you're not really taking it seriously

Progress against your growth strategy needs to be a regular and high-priority item on any Exco agenda. This simple discipline will ensure alignment, provision of necessary resources/support, and an appropriate challenge to your designated Growth Director. Don't ignore growth; nothing you do as an Exco is more important. If growth rarely appears as an Exco agenda item (and this is the case in many companies) then you can be sure it is not getting the senior management attention that it needs.

As you would expect, some businesses are already operating like this – and are growing strongly as a result. We discuss a number of these case studies within the book and contrast them with the fortunes of companies who have not yet learned how to bake in in Good Growth habits.

There are many fewer businesses enjoying Good Growth than there should be. And that's a shame.

If you want to understand how to hardwire your organisation for Good Growth, then read on.

You might just find out what the Growth Director has got to be so secretive about . . .

Case Study: Organisation structure drives effective growth strategy – DFS and Boots; *Ian Filby, Chief Executive Officer, DFS*

Ian Filby has been CEO of DFS, the market-leading furniture retailer since September 2010. Under Ian's leadership, DFS has weathered the downturn in the UK economy to deliver strong, profitable growth, with gross sales up 7%, and Earnings Before Interest, Taxes, Depreciation and Amortisation (EBITDA) up +8.4% in financial year (FY) 2015.

Prior to leading DFS, Ian worked at Boots, latterly in an Exco role as buying director for the beauty and toiletries business, which accounts for around 60% of Boots' annual profit.

We asked Ian to talk about what he had learned about creating organisational structures and cultures focused on delivering significant, sustained, profitable growth.

'I spent almost 30 years at Boots, with most of the last ten of those in a leadership position on the Boots Exco.

During my time leading the Boots Beauty business, I was doing a lot of learning on the job – and, although we did succeed in generating some significant growth over time, it would be wrong to say we started with a clear strategy. Rather, we had a general idea of the themes we wanted to pursue. I worked hard to put in place a genuinely talented team of leaders and, partly through smart planning and partly, frankly, through trial and error, we were able to identify and bring to market initiatives that built the business.

What worked well for us was that we built an excellent, competitive but collaborative culture which caused the best initiatives to be prioritised, and, because of my time in the business, I understood how to get things done in the Boots organisation.

When I became Chief Executive at DFS, however, I knew that a more thoughtful approach would be needed. DFS had just been bought by the private equity company, Advent (I had helped with the due diligence ahead of the transaction) and, like all Private Equity (P/E) owners, they were sure to be very focused on a fast return on their investment.

It was clear to me that the team knew how to run the DFS business – they did not need my help there. Where I could add value, though, was by creating what they had previously lacked – a clear strategy for ahead-of-market growth, and an organisational design to deliver it.

The due diligence process, and some early strategy consultation work by Bain and Company had given me all the analysis, views of opportunities and risks, and options for alternative routes ahead that I needed.

Armed with these, I spent three days away from the business crafting a simple, coherent strategy for growth that I could use as a basis for discussion with the business on the way forward.

The key elements of this strategy were quite simple, but very powerful.

Firstly, there was real clarity about where our sources of growth were going to come from. The analysis had segmented our customer base into five groups, and we understood very clearly not only where the best growth opportunities were, but also what an x% increase in penetration of each group would deliver for us. Pushing the organisation to focus on the consumers with greatest growth potential was crucial to optimising use of our resources and delivering growth cost-effectively.

Second, we identified four Strategic Activity Pillars that would drive the initiatives necessary to deliver growth. These covered customer targeting; value; multi-channel retailing; and brand personality. All initiatives that made it to market HAD to emerge from one of these four pillars or we would not prioritise them.

Third, we set the organisation up to deliver BOTH against the short-term sales/profit targets that drive all retailers, and against the longer-term strategic initiatives that will ensure continued/accelerating growth in the years ahead. To do this I set up two executive board meetings: an operating board that met bi-weekly to 'run the business' and a smaller strategy development board that met monthly and focused on delivering the stretch goals set out in the strategic growth plan.

Finally, and crucially, we changed the way we assessed our leadership team so that everyone had four or five strategic priorities as part of their personal assessment goals, as well as the shorter-term target that had previously been the team's priority. It's amazing how the focus changes according to what you bonus people on!

The impact of this plan has been significant. By ensuring we had a plan that everyone understood and bought into, we suddenly raised the organisation's eyes from 'delivering this year's numbers' to 'hitting our stretch long-term growth targets' – a much more ambitious mindset.

By creating organisational structures that forced a regular focus on the growth strategy and by linking individuals' personal assessments to it we made growth a regular focus for the Executive team.

By starting with real clarity on which consumers to prioritise for growth, we found ourselves much more able to prioritise initiatives and focus resources on those most likely to deliver the growth we needed.

Without realising it, we also effectively created a Growth Director position. We call it Online and Customer Strategy Director – but I think it's pretty much the same thing.

And the results have illustrated the power of this approach. Despite significant market decline (due to the post-financial crisis impacts on consumer spending), we have been able to meet all the financial goals set at the time the business was acquired. We have consistently out-grown the market, and currently target to double the prevailing rate of market growth over the next planning cycle. Growth strategy in action!

My point, really, is that organisations need to force themselves to step back from all the day-to-day madness, work out how they intend to grow, and then ensure they are structuring, resourcing and incentivising their teams appropriately. In my experience – it pays off!'

Case Study: Barclays Bank: Building radically different structures to empower growth; *Ashok Vaswani, Chief Executive Officer, Barclays' Retail and Business Bank*

One of the most unusual – and yet also most effective – examples of building an organisational structure to deliver growth that I have seen was driven by Ashok Vaswani, the CEO of Barclays' Retail and Business Bank.

Ashok had a deep-seated belief that growth can only be delivered by organisations that are not only focused against 'How do we grow?' but also where everyone can feel complete ownership of the strategies to deliver this growth. In large organisations that tend (despite fine words to the contrary) to default to a 'command and control' structure, where the executives develop strategies for the organisation to deliver, this can be incredibly difficult to achieve. Yet Ashok did exactly that at Barclays, using some truly innovative thinking, radically different organisational structures, and a genuine willingness to devolve decision making to levels below his executive team of direct reports.

'The first step for any organisation is to truly believe that growth is possible, and to understand that, to achieve it, they may have to move away from the management structures and strategic approaches with which they are familiar.

As CEO, I see my role as setting a clear direction, but then being prepared to let go and allow colleagues to develop and implement the strategies and plans to deliver the growth we need. So I wanted to do two key things.

The first was to find a set of clear principles that would enable us to move in a common direction. The second was to find a way to break down departmental silos.

In setting a clear course, I decided not to differentiate via new banking products – the regulatory barriers to doing things radically differently were just too high. Instead, we would aim to differentiate ourselves by changing the way customers could interact with our bank. But that's as far as I wanted my direction to go.

So, I set up a large number of teams across the business, involving colleagues from the most junior to the most senior (including the recent graduates – some of the smartest ideas came from the most junior people) and asked them to brainstorm ways in which we could radically differentiate customer interactions, and try to turn these into the outline of a business strategy.

The results were amazing. Simply being asked to work on strategy by the new CEO was hugely empowering for people – the levels of energy and number of ideas were incredible. Out of this work a quite radical and highly effective new operating strategy was developed.

But to achieve a true transformation of the way we worked needed a complete elimination of silos. Words alone would never accomplish this. So we decided to break down departmental barriers by setting up cross-functional 'Councils', and gave them responsibility for different areas of the business – so, we had a Consumer Lending Council; a Mortgages Council; a Business Banking Council, and so on.

Each Council was led by a member of the executive team, and was made up of representatives from each of the key departments in the business – Finance, Operations, IT, HR, Product Development, Marketing, etc. The Council had responsibility for managing its area of operation as a stand-alone business, with a P&L for which they were accountable.

At a stroke, this broke down the traditional departmental barriers and focused people on delivering against the needs of our customers. It empowered the organisation to be accountable for the commitments it had made – no more expecting the Chief Executive to tell it what to do.

The results were significant. In three years we built PBT from around £1.1bn to £1.7bn – growth of around 50%. A wonderful example of what people in businesses can achieve – if their organisations let them.'

In my experience the willingness of Ashok and his executive team at Barclays to delegate decision making to the cross-functional Councils is a most unusual example of senior executives being prepared to let go in order to empower their organisations and release the latent drive and creativity of their people. Paradoxically, the larger the organisation, the greater tends to be the compulsion of senior management to try to control things from the centre.

Barclays' willingness to trust its teams, and to devolve responsibility for both strategic direction and day-to-day decision-making (within a framework that Ashok and the executive team had set), released huge energy and delivered impressive growth results in the incredibly difficult operating climate that existed for UK banks after the financial services crash of 2008.

The Big Growth Mistake: The fundamental misunderstandings that cause many businesses to struggle to grow

Chapter 1 established that organisational structures, the lack of clear executive accountability and focus, and the tendency towards investment-averse cultures are often real hindrances to the efforts of many good businesses to grow. If your business has these organizational issues – then fix them. You're unlikely to be able to grow sustainably unless you do.

But – there is a much more fundamental barrier preventing many companies delivering significant, sustained, profitable 'Good Growth'.

The Growth Director says:
Don't forget, 'Good Growth' is the *only* sort of growth worth having.

'Good Growth' means:

- growth driven by 'recruiting' more consumers through a preferred proposition – not through 'buying' consumers with promotional/pricing activity;
- growth driven by increased penetration of your market – not by relying on the same small group of 'super-users';
- proposition-driven growth that delivers increased loyalty from existing users;
- users happy to buy at full price – reduced reliance on price/promotional spend;
- users who are active advocates for your brand – and whose enthusiasm recruits others; and
- growth that is likely to drive top line and margin up, costs down, and, of course, bottom line profit strongly upwards.

This is a fundamental mistake that most companies make in their assumptions about how consumers shop, make purchase decisions and choose between brands. This leads many companies to construct commercial and marketing plans that are complex, expensive and overly reliant on promotions and price cutting to sustain short-term sales. Most importantly, despite all the effort that goes into them and all the money they cost to develop and run, the commercial plans of many companies do not deliver significant, sustained, profitable growth.

Think that might apply to the commercial plans run in your business? Well see how many of these common symptoms of such ineffective commercial activity you recognise:

- 'Always on' promotional plans?
- Flip-flopping advertising campaigns? (How long has your current campaign been on air?)
- Increasingly expensive retailer support programmes? (Don't these inevitably get more expensive year after year?)
- A blizzard of new initiatives . . . many of which don't work?
- Increasingly complex media plans?
- Short-term sales overly dependent on pricing?

Growth is difficult. Investors, shareholders, impatient boards and demanding retailers and distributors put huge pressure on companies to deliver. This pushes management teams into developing complex and expensive commercial and marketing strategies in order to show they are 'doing stuff'.

But, all too often, and despite all of the effort and cost put into developing and implementing such strategies and plans, the fact remains that most companies fail to grow significantly and sustainably because their plans are often built on a fundamental misunderstanding about how consumers shop, make purchase decisions and choose between brands.

This is what we call the Big Growth Mistake. We believe it is the fundamental reason for the existence of the paradox we introduced in Chapter 1: that despite its incredible importance, most companies fail to deliver significant, sustained, profitable growth. What is The Big Growth Mistake? Why is it so important? And why has no-one noticed it until now?

The Big Growth Mistake that most companies make is simply this: They assume that all consumer purchases are up for grabs – they're not.

The implicit assumption behind the commercial plans of most companies is that every consumer purchase in their category is potentially available to them – and that the job of their commercial plan is to grab as many of these purchases as possible. With this defining assumption, companies inevitably default to constructing 'super busy' commercial plans that are desperately trying to get the attention of every potential consumer ahead of every purchase they make to persuade/cajole/pressurise them into switching to their brand.

Companies making this assumption will inevitably persuade themselves that, if every purchase occasion out there is up for grabs, then obviously we need 'always on' promotional plans; we need to ensure we are always securing prime promotional space from each of our key retailers; we need to get our advertising messages out there with high frequency – and with plenty of good 'buy us now!' elements in each of them; and we need to keep attracting the attention of our potential purchasers by bringing a stream of new ideas to market – just in case it was the lack of that fifth fragrance or 20% extra limited edition pack that was stopping them from buying us.

Think we're exaggerating the extent to which typical commercial plans are built in this way? Take a look at these.

Most brands are over-reliant on promotional activity

Here's data from in-store research in the UK on the incidence of promotional activity in a range of typical consumer product categories:

Product category	SKUs on promotion (Feb 2016)
Laundry detergents – liquids	71%
Cereals	19%
Crisps	61%
Fizzy drinks – cans	38%
Squash drinks	76%
Sweet biscuits	50%
Yoghurts	73%

Data taken from in-store research in UK supermarkets; February 2016.

While this is a snapshot of data, it is a typical picture familiar to anyone who shops regularly in supermarkets. Further, what this data does not show is that the brands not on promotion when this data was taken would almost certainly be on offer in the next promotional cycle – some two–four weeks later. This almost inevitably makes the impact of any single promotion short-term in nature – any gains from competitors while you are on promotion will be lost during the next promotion cycle when your competitor is on offer. Later in this chapter we share some compelling data on the ineffectiveness of promotions produced by Byron Sharp in his book *How Brands Grow*.

Brands over-rely on new initiatives – and most don't work

Here's some data showing the percentage of SKUs in the same consumer product categories that are variants of the original core brand (e.g. different flavours or different pack sizes). While this does not tell the whole 'new initiative' story – and while some of these variants (e.g. diet colas) have become as established as the 'mother' brand) it does give an indication of the extent to which brands rely on new variants, new sizes or other new initiatives to drive growth.

Product category	SKUs that are new variants
Laundry detergents – liquids	79%
Cereals	78%
Crisps	86%
Fizzy drinks – cans	59%
Squash drinks	71%
Sweet biscuits	63%
Yoghurts	78%

Data taken from in-store research in UK supermarkets; February 2016.

Perhaps this would not matter if new initiatives reliably drove growth. But this is not the case. Much data exists on the failure rate of new initiatives: Inez Blackburn and her team at the University of Toronto in 2008 concluded the failure rate of new initiatives was 80%. Even more strikingly, a McKinsey Global Innovation Survey in 2015 found that only 6% of companies were satisfied with their innovation performance – and furthermore, 'very few executives know what the problem is and how to improve in innovation and R&D'. This is, of course, a particular concern for companies because of the cost and increased complexity involved in bringing new initiatives to market – and yet this chronic under-performance persists.

Of course, if all this effort and expense was reliably driving sustainable and profitable growth for the businesses involved, then you might argue it was all worth it. But, as we saw in Chapter 1, very few companies are delivering significant, sustainable, profitable Good Growth.

> ### *The Growth Director says:*
> The Big Growth Mistake is the fundamental error preventing companies from growing as significantly, sustainably and profitably as they desire.
>
> - The Big Growth Mistake is to assume that all consumer purchases in your category are up for grabs – they're not.
> - Because of this mistake most companies construct 'super-busy' commercial plans in an attempt to grab as big a share of category purchases as possible.
> - Symptoms of this mistake are: 'always on' promotional plans; price used as a lever to drive sales; 'flip-flopping' marketing and advertising campaigns; 'new initiative-itis'; escalating costs of securing retailer/ distributor support; complex, expensive media plans
> - Most of this expensive activity is simply 'zoned out' and ignored.

Underlying this data, of course, is the reality that despite all those manic efforts to secure their attention and attract their preference, consumers in most categories seem very resistant to switching brands.

Why are consumers not open to switching brands every time they go shopping? After all, don't we all want to make sensible choices about the brands that are best for us, taking into account brand reputation, performance claims, look of the packaging, price and promotional offer? Well – yes we do. And in a perfect world we might indeed evaluate every purchase decision carefully. But, usually, we simply don't have time.

Its been estimated that, in a typical day, a western consumer will encounter anywhere from 500 to 5,000 advertising and promotional messages – the numbers vary hugely depending on whose study you are using, but even at the lowest end of the estimates they are all pretty significant! If we had nothing else to do but evaluate alternative consumer products this would already be far too many for us even to begin to consider. Given that most of us have more important things to think about (family, friends, work, social life, crucial upcoming televised sporting events …), it would be hugely inefficient for us to try to engage with all but a tiny proportion of these messages.

Over the millennia, our brains have worked this out and have hard-wired us to cut through the incredible complexity of our lives by operating, most of the time, on 'autopilot'.

Our 'autopilot' systems work subconsciously and govern around 90%–95% of the choices we make in every area of our lives.

Chapter 4 of this book explains in a lot more detail how our autopilot decision-making processes work – but the crucial point is that they drive the vast majority of the purchases we make – and they operate subconsciously. As we operate on autopilot for the vast majority of the time, we are just not open to considering purchase of brands other than the small portfolio of favourites that we have (subconsciously) chosen as our autopilots. Put simply, life is just too short for us to consider the vast majority of marketing and promotional messages we are bombarded with daily. And that's quite shocking for many companies given how much time and money is poured into trying to get attention and consideration from potential consumers and to persuade them to switch from their usual brand.

Of course, some companies might accept this analysis as being accurate – but would still be reluctant to acknowledge that their commercial plans are as wasteful as our autopilot observations imply. Well – we think they may be slightly fooling themselves, and are guilty of underestimating just how smart (and powerful) our sub-conscious brains are.

If you doubt whether you are operating on autopilot most of the time, try answering these two simple questions:

- How many TV channels do you have access to on your television?
- How many of these channels account for 75% or more of your viewing?

Unless you're very unusual, you will have answered 'around 150' to the first question and '3 to 5' to the second.

So – why is that? Surely if you took the trouble, the chances are that at almost any time you could find a more attractive programme on one of the channels you visit less frequently? Well yes, you probably could. But, it would take an awful lot of time and mental energy to scroll through all those channels and evaluate all your options. And, because you don't want to spend your time in this way, your brain will at some point have decided, subconsciously, that your three or four favourites are quite likely to meet most of your TV viewing needs most of the time – and so you automatically default to these channels every time you turn the television on. Alternatives are very rarely considered.

Taking a good friend as an example of this (OK, it's me . . .), almost all my TV viewing is taken up by just three channels: BBC1, BBC2 and Sky Sports. Classic autopilot. Without ever thinking consciously about it, I default to my three favourite channels almost every time I switch on the television. It's an incredibly sensible way to maximise use of my time. Yet I was never aware of deciding to behave like this.

If this is how we behave in a situation where evaluation of alternatives is as easy and cost-free as flicking from channel to channel by remote control, how much more will this behaviour drive our decision making when it comes to purchasing relatively expensive consumer products? That's how the autopilot works.

Autopilot behaviour driving our shopping decisions has been understood and reported on extensively in the academic world for many years. Here are observations from a few of the more authoritative studies:

> Buyers restrict their purchases to a personal repertoire of brands . . . buyers keep returning to their favourites, and their set of favourites can be very small.

> Sharp (2010)

American families tend to buy the same products repeatedly . . . products that meet 85% of their household needs.

Ries and Trout (1981)

So – our autopilots are switched on all the time – and they always have been.

The quote from Jack Trout above is taken from a book first published in the 1960s – it really is quite surprising that a phenomenon so well recognised by the academic world for so many years has not made more impact with business leaders and organisations. I guess we've all been too busy . . .

Our own studies have followed purchasing behaviour in a large number of consumer markets – and again we observe very consistent autopilot behaviour dominating purchase patterns in every one – consumers buy their favourite product with great consistency. Occasionally, they may make a one-off purchase from a competitor (usually in response to a promotional offer or lack of availability of their autopilot brand) but then they invariably return to their autopilot on the next shopping occasion. Later in this chapter we present some interesting – and for many companies very worrying – data on the lack of effectiveness of promotional activity in changing autopilot choice.

The Growth Director says:

Most of the time, most consumers shop on autopilot from a small portfolio of favourite brands.

- These autopilot brands have been chosen subconsciously; consumers feel an emotional bond with them and, once chosen, they are rarely changed.
- In consumer product categories, autopilot purchases account for 75–90% of a consumer's category shopping.
- Because our brains have hard-wired us to operate on autopilot most of the time we 'tune out' all other approaches from other brands – most of the time we fail to even notice competing brands' attempts to win our business.
- The key to growth is to learn how to become the default autopilot choice for the consumers in your targeted category – that's it.

So – it seems clear that autopilot shopping dominates our purchasing behaviour – and the neuroscientific reasons for our being hard-wired to behave this way make instinctive sense. But why does missing this truth – in effect, making the Big Growth Mistake – matter so much to companies trying to develop commercial plans to grow their businesses?

Well, it's simply that while the autopilot phenomenon shows us that the vast majority of purchase decisions are just not available to other brands, most companies' commercial and marketing plans seem to take no account of this, and appear to be striving to attract the attention of every passing consumer in every purchase situation in the hope that some of them will be persuaded to switch.

The data shown earlier in this chapter illustrated clearly how companies have become overly reliant on 'always on' promotional plans, a deluge of new initiatives (most of which do not work) and frequently changing marketing and advertising campaigns. Given the fact of autopilot shopping, commercial plans built and executed in this way just do not make sense. In the vast majority of occasions the consumers reached by these messages/initiatives are just not listening and will not change their behaviour, which means that most of the time and money devoted to developing and implementing these activities is simply wasted.

> . . . there is little evidence that . . . price cuts attract new customers to buy a brand. Ehrenberg, Hammond and Goodhardt (1994) found that almost everyone who bought a brand during a price promotion had bought the brand previously.
>
> Sharp (2010)

Let's look at that last sentence again: '. . . almost everyone who bought during a price promotion had bought the brand previously'. Wow! That's certainly not what the company intended, but, we'd say, incredibly clear evidence of the power of autopilot shopping behaviour. Price cuts may boost sales temporarily by bringing forward purchases from shoppers who have already chosen you as their autopilot brand – but have little or no impact on consumers who have chosen other brands as their autopilot. You could say that's rather a waste of money.

Similarly, Sharp (2010) looked at whether high-impact promotional offers were effective at bringing new shoppers into a brand's portfolio.

What has been found is that a price promotion pulls in a large proportion of infrequent buyers. They buy during the promotion and then afterwards resume their low buying propensity. In other words after the promotional purchase it is as if nothing happened.

Sharp (2010)

Again, we'd say that's clear evidence of autopilot at work. Even if high-profile promotions temporarily 'rent' some purchases from non-autopilot shoppers, those shoppers revert to their usual autopilot brand as soon as the promotion is over.

Neither of these examples seem to be very cost-effective ways of deploying commercial/marketing funds – and neither should be expected to deliver sustained growth. We think most companies know this. Most CEOs, pretty much all chief financial officers (CFOs), and a fair proportion of chief marketing officers (CMOs) know, deep down, that an awful lot of the money they spend on their commercial and marketing plans is not driving the growth they desire.

A simple metric to illustrate this is the frequency with which major companies change their marketing/advertising campaigns. Clearly, if a campaign was driving the desired growth, then it would remain unchanged. Think of the longevity of obviously successful campaigns such as Fairy Liquid's 'mother and child/mildness' campaigns of the 1960s–1980s and Fosters' 'The Amber Nectar' campaign of the 1980s and 1990s to more recently successful campaigns like Lynx's 'Lynx Effect' or Tesco's 'Every Little Helps', both of which drove these brands to sustained growth in the 2000s.

But those campaigns are not typical. Most brands, unfortunately, seem to find it very hard to stick to an advertising campaign for much longer than a year at a time. To illustrate this I've taken the example of how major brands often change campaigns around their Christmas marketing. Just look at how few of the expensively marketed brands shown below maintained consistency in their Christmas marketing campaigns (note: 'change' here does NOT include campaigns where the core idea stayed the same but the execution changed from one year to the next – that would count as a 'no change' result).

Brand	Campaign idea Christmas 2014	Campaign idea Christmas 2015	Change or not?
John Lewis	Tear-jerking story of buying a special gift (little boy for his toy penguin)	Tear-jerking story of buying special gift (little girl for Man on the Moon)	No change
Tesco	Celebratory 'Turn Lights on for Christmas' ad	Series of comedic 'slice of life' ads set in-store	Different campaigns
M&S	Spectacular fantasy story ('Magic and Sparkle' fairies)	Studio-shot, high-impact showcase for Christmas product range	Different campaigns
Boots	Tear-jerking story of family coming together at Christmas	High-impact product showcase ad	Different campaigns
Coke	Coke Truck signalling 'Christmas is here'	'Event ad' encouraging people to 'Share The Good'	Different campaigns
Cadbury's	Series of improvised celebrity sketches	Cadbury's Trucks 'spreading the joy' across the UK	Different campaigns

Given the time, money and expertise put into developing each year's Christmas campaign, it is remarkable how quickly these major brands abandon their work. Notably, the one retailer who has stuck with a consistent campaign idea for many years – John Lewis – is the regular 'winner' of the Christmas sales battle. While you might argue that the special nature of Christmas makes these changes more likely, this surprising reluctance to stick with campaigns even from one year to the next is all too common. Far too frequently marketing and advertising campaigns are changed on a 12–18 month cycle – often without any real understanding of whether or not they have been effective. Here are some concurring expert views.

Today's advertising campaigns are fleeting: here today, gone tomorrow.

Blocki (2015)

Marketers abandon new advertising without knowing whether or not it's effective.

Swalek (2013)

That constant churn in marketing campaigns tells you something. It tells you that the companies concerned decided their campaigns weren't working – in effect, that they were failing to deliver sufficient growth. We think this behaviour is very common across very many consumer-facing businesses.

Here's the views of someone with many years of experience of this. David Gray is a founding partner of Creative Leap, a leading UK Marketing and Branding Agency. David has helped brands from a range of sectors position themselves for growth. His experience includes working on brands like Boots, Barclays, Bupa, Johnson & Johnson and Reckitt Benckiser.

Here, David describes the frustrations of working on businesses whose commercial plans, and marketing strategies, have suffered from making the Big Growth Mistake.

Case Study: The Big Growth Mistake Drives Commercial Ineffectiveness; *by David Gray, Founding Partner Creative Leap*

'There is no doubt that the executive teams of many of the companies that I have been associated with have felt under great pressure to deliver short-term sales results. Some sectors are more focused on the short-term than others – retailers, famously, worry if they experience just a few days of below-expectation sales – but in almost all businesses you feel the pressure to deliver this week's/this month's/this quarter's numbers as a huge priority.

And there is no doubt that this can often lead to marketing and advertising activity that is overly short term in nature.

Often, rather than a considered evaluation of how to position their brands to maximise their attractiveness to the highest-potential consumers, many businesses act as if they need to try to 'grab' as many of the available purchases as they possibly can via commercial plans that prioritise short-term tactical activity over longer-term brand-building.

For advertising and marketing agencies, who are particularly motivated by building stronger, more attractive brands, this can sometimes be frustrating. And, in my opinion, this is often a reason why many businesses find it difficult to deliver sustainable growth over time. There are probably two common manifestations of this behaviour that cause the agency world particular frustration:

The first of these, particularly prevalent in the world of retailing, is the reliance on large numbers of price-driven or offer-driven ads – often placed in newspapers. The logic, of course, is that these enable companies to showcase their best offers and drive consumers into store for the weekly shop. The paradox is that, since all retailers use very similar tactics, and since they ensure that their offers are as good as their competitors, these ads often simply cancel each other out. These price-driven campaigns can be very expensive to place (prime position in national newspapers does not come cheap) and often drive a lot of internal costs for retailers as they move this week's special offers into prime position in store.

But – retailers feel good if they see their ads loud and proud in the national papers – and it does definitely satisfy an exco need to 'do stuff', so a lot of money is spent on campaigns like these. They certainly do little for the long-term health of the brands concerned, and agencies do get frustrated that so much of the available money is spent on essentially short-term activity. But most retail cultures just 'feel better' with lots of price or promotions-driven advertising out there – it's a very hard habit to break.

The second manifestation of this 'grab for growth' approach that I would draw attention to is the cycle that many companies in all sectors go through of searching for the 'magic advertising campaign' that will transform their fortunes. The cycle reminds me a lot of the way that football teams change their managers: a new guy is recruited, often at great pace and with little real thought as to his suitability; huge excitement and anticipation follows; he is given lots of money to spend in the transfer market, and does so; the team initially respond to the freshness of his approach and results temporarily improve; after a while the team experiences a bad patch, fans and the owner get impatient and the manager is sacked. The whole cycle then starts again.

There is a similar 'new advertising campaign' cycle in many companies, with characteristics not unlike those of the football club recruiting its next manager. Companies often brief new campaigns when they are experiencing a period of poor growth. Rather than examine the fundamentals of their proposition, they tend to believe that they just need new advertising. The campaign will be briefed quite quickly and with huge expectations, but often with little in the way of fresh consumer insights to justify a new approach. Production costs for the new campaign will be very high and expectations of its impact will be significant. Initially positive results (often down to all the extra promotional activity in support of the campaign launch) will flatten after a while, and, before long, the feeling will be that the campaign has failed. Cue search for the next one – sometimes with a new marketing director or advertising agency! Again, this hyperactive cycle satisfies a management desire to 'do stuff' to grab consumers' attention and drive growth – but is often poorly thought through and, however well executed, is not likely to make a lasting impact on growth.

In my opinion businesses would benefit hugely from resisting the urge to rush to action, and to take the time to consider how thoughtful repositioning of their brands is likely to deliver much more significant and lasting growth. This type of patience can sometimes be a rare commodity at the top of consumer businesses!'

Typically, as companies pass through the cycle that David describes, they will blame their executional plans for lack of results. This not only results in prematurely junking expensively developed campaigns, but also, often, to dispensing with the services of their advertising agency or (shriek!) their marketing director.

But – maybe it wasn't the execution that was at fault at all. Maybe the reason that so many commercial plans and marketing campaigns fail to deliver growth is because they are built on that Big Growth Mistake – the fundamental misunderstanding of how consumers shop, make purchase decisions and choose between brands. Maybe without addressing this fundamental issue it is almost certain that most campaigns, most of the time, will disappoint. The few that do turn out to be successful will have 'got lucky' and will prove very hard to reproduce.

That might lead us to conclude that, if autopilot shopping is the default behaviour that we are all hard-wired to follow, then maybe the key question companies should be asking themselves is not 'How can I shout a little louder/more effectively than my competitors?' but rather 'What do I need to do to make my brand the dominant autopilot in my category?'

By the way – that second question is much the harder one to answer. Its what the next chapters of this book go on to address.

Case Study: 'New Coke': Was It the Definitive Example of The Big Growth Mistake?; *Phil Anderton, Global Brand Manager Coca Cola 1996–1998*

Phil Anderton started his career at Procter and Gamble, leaving to join Coca-Cola in the mid 1990s. He spent two-and-a-half years as Global Brand Manager and also worked for Coca-Cola in Europe before building a career in the sports world including roles as CMO of the ATP World Tour and CEO roles at Scottish Rugby, Hearts FC and Al Jazira.

While at Coca-Cola, Phil observed at first hand how the Big Growth Mistake can afflict even the biggest, most successful companies in the world.

'Back in the 1990s, mighty Coca Cola (Coke) was struggling. Sales and market share had been flat or declining for a number of years. Coke, once the cool, youthful, aspirational brand that had 'Taught The World To Sing' in the 1970s had become stodgy, dull and unfashionable.

In contrast, that cocky upstart Pepsi had become the brand the cool people identified with. Pepsi had targeted a youthful consumer, had associated itself with rebellious sports stars like Shaquille O'Neal with edgy(ish) musicians like Michael Jackson and was the brand the cool kids (and therefore all the middle aged people who wanted to be thought of as still being 'down with tha' cool kids) wanted to drink. Their tag line was that Pepsi was 'The Choice of a New Generation' – and, for a while, it was.

Between the late 1970s and the early 1990s Pepsi built share by over 50%, reaching a US share over 30% and bringing the share gap with Coke to below 10% points.

But Pepsi's cool image wasn't the worst thing for its struggling rivals at Coke – the Pepsi marketing machine trumpeted how much, in blind taste tests, consumers consistently preferred their product to Coke . . . and ran campaign after campaign of the 'Pepsi Taste Test' on television just to remind people of this fact – and rub Coke's corporate noses in this unpalatable truth.

So how does a struggling mega-brand react when threatened in this way?

Well they would probably have been best advised to step back, take a breath and go back to basics – reminding themselves of who their target consumers were and what they wanted, identifying why these people had fallen out of love with them and addressing, carefully but speedily, the one or two controlling elements of their proposition that could have turned their fortunes around.

But, of course, as for most companies struggling against resurgent competitors this feels like procrastination at best, paralysis at worst. The Big Growth Mistake always drives action over thoughtfulness. Exec teams of struggling mega-brands demand ACTION! Get out there and do – STUFF! Whatever it takes to cuff those upstarts from Pepsi and get our consumers back. We don't care what it is – JUST DO SOMETHING!

And that's exactly what they did at Coke in the late 1980s and early 1990s . . . Stuff . . . and then more Stuff.

They stepped up their advertising spend . . . desperately trying to appeal to the younger consumers that Pepsi had won over with iteration after iteration of the 'Have a Coke and a Smile' campaign. The approach seemed to be: 'No-ones listening to us any more – SHOUT LOUDER!'

Pepsi secured some smart and very effective sponsorships with youth-oriented properties including extensive sponsorship of the radio music charts in the US. So Coke's reaction had to be 'Get Out There And Sponsor Stuff!'. You may suspect I'm exaggerating, but as just one example of this rather manic behaviour – in 1993 in the UK alone, Coke had over 30 sponsorships (that's right – over 30!), including (wait for it . . .) the Chelsea Flower Show!

And, in a desperate effort to keep retailers onside, Coke went initiative crazy, rolling into the market special pack after special pack and initiative after initiative including such ill-judged and short-term ideas as Vanilla Coke and Tab Clear.

But, most damaging of all, Pepsi's success and Coke's increasingly desperate (and unsuccessful) attempts to find an effective way to fight back led them to one of the all-time-great business errors – changing the

Coke formula in a doomed attempt to ape the (sweeter) taste that Pepsi offered with the introduction of New Coke in the late 1980s.

So desperate were Coke to stop Pepsi's growth that they abandoned their unique, authentic, decades-old formula and moved to a new taste much closer to that of their recently successful rivals. The perceived need to move quickly, and the sense of 'we MUST take action' that the commercial pressure that they felt engendered meant that pre-launch research was overly focused on non/occasional/Pepsi users and missed the hugely important truth that, while Coke loyalists quite liked the taste of New Coke as an occasional alternative, they did NOT want their traditional Coke replaced on a permanent basis.

And, as New Coke hit the market, with huge (and hugely expensive marketing fanfare) they expressed their opinions forcibly. The reaction of Coke loyalists was powerful and angry. Not only were they reluctant to buy New Coke but they deluged US media, and the Coca-Cola PR department with howls of outrage and demands to get their 'old' Coke back.

'Horrible!'

Of course, the company responded and, as quickly as it was able, reversed the change to its formula and reintroduced its classic Coke product. But this was not only hugely damaging to the brand (and very embarrassing for the management team) but also extremely costly and disruptive for the whole organisation. What a powerful example of the organisational 'madness' that The Big Growth Mistake can induce.'

It's just worth pausing to consider these results. Coca-Cola had upped its marketing spend, increased its promotional frequency and cost, thrown money at retailers to secure their preferential support, sponsored almost anything that moved, driven into the market waves of costly initiatives that added cost and complexity to their business, and finally changed the formula that had delivered unprecedented success to their business over decades – and still they struggled to grow.

New Coke is an extreme example – but this case study does illustrate very powerfully how the assumption that the answer to 'How Do We

Grow?' is 'Do Stuff ... Quickly!' almost always drives expensive, wasteful and counter-productive activity.

The Big Growth Mistake blights the prospects of so many companies.

The story of how Coca-Cola recovered, went back to basics, worked out how to reposition itself and won back all of that lost share is a compelling one – and is recounted elsewhere in this book. For now, we should all take Coke's experience to heart. If even the mighty Coca-Cola Corporation can make the Big Growth Mistake – then we all can.

The Growth Director's Summary

- **The Big Growth Mistake** that most companies make is to assume that all consumer purchases in their category are up for grabs: they're not.
- Because of this, most companies construct 'super busy' commercial plans in a desperate attempt to grab as big a share of category purchases as possible.
- Symptoms are: 'always on' promotional plans; price used as a lever to drive sales; 'flip-flopping' marketing and advertising campaigns; 'new initiative-itis'; escalating costs of securing retailer/distributor support; and complex, expensive media plans.
- In fact, most of the time, consumers shop on autopilot from a small portfolio of favourite brands. These have been chosen subconsciously; consumers feel an emotional bond with them and, once chosen, these brands are rarely changed – typically they will account for 75–90% of a consumer's category purchases.
- Because our brains have 'hard-wired' us to operate on autopilot so we 'tune out' all other approaches from other brands – most of the time we fail to even notice competing brands' attempts to win our business.
- This means that, unfortunately, there is huge wastage in the commercial and marketing plans of most brands – the consumers they are aimed at are simply not listening.
- The ultimate consequence of all this wasted commercial effort is, of course, that most brands are unable to deliver significant, sustained, profitable growth.

Chapter 3

The New Growth Paradigm: A radical new way for companies to approach the challenge of generating significant, sustainable, profitable growth

OK – pay attention: this is a very important chapter. This is where you start to get an idea of what it is that really drives growth – a first glimpse into what the Growth Director's secret really is.

Chapter 2 established that our brains have 'hardwired' us to shop on autopilot almost all the time, choosing from a small portfolio of favourite brands/products that we have chosen subconsciously. We are hard-wired to screen out 'noise' from brands other than our favourites (Note: I'm afraid that, in this case, 'noise' probably includes all of your carefully constructed marketing plans …) and to default to our autopilots on almost all shopping occasions.

Failure to understand this truth about how we operate is the Big Growth Mistake that can blight the commercial planning of most companies, and lead to huge wastage on ineffective commercial, product and marketing plans which simply do not deliver the significant, sustained growth that they were designed to achieve.

The key to Good Growth – significant, sustained, profitable growth – is simply this: you must learn how to become the default autopilot brand for your target consumers in the category/sub-category in which you operate.

Once secured, autopilot status will deliver 75%+ of the purchases of your 'converted' consumers, it will build an army of highly motivated advocates who will influence others to make you their autopilot, and it will recruit more and more of your target customers to your brand on a week–by–week basis. As a very attractive additional benefit, becoming the default autopilot choice will also reduce your dependency on expensive promotions/price cuts/retailer support programmes; consumers buying on autopilot are happy to buy at full price as well as when your brand is discounted. That means that your growth is also likely to be profitable. You might wish to point this out to your CFO . . .

In effect, securing dominant autopilot status means that significant, sustained, profitable growth will be effectively baked-in to the way your business/brand operates. Who wouldn't want that?

The Growth Director says:

The key to Good Growth is becoming the dominant autopilot brand in your category . . . that's it.

- Our brains have hard-wired us to shop on autopilot from a small portfolio of favourite brands . . . most of the time we pay no attention to the efforts of other brands to secure our business
- Once secured, autopilot status delivers 75%+ of the purchases of your converted consumers and will recruit more and more target customers month after month, year after year
- Autopilot brands are likely to be much more profitable since consumers on autopilot will buy at full price and will stay loyal with much less marketing/promotional effort than other consumers.

But . . . securing autopilot status is not easy.

This chapter describes what it takes to secure autopilot status. Subsequent chapters deconstruct each element of this so that you can understand how this thinking should be applied in your business. Before we get into this, and without worrying yet about how these brands became autopilot choices, let's look at the impact that attaining that status has had on a few well-known businesses.

Autopilot example: Lynx deodorant/ bodyspray

Back in the mid-1990s, Lynx was a worn-out brand that nobody wanted to buy – the Chairman of its advertising agency famously described the 1990s Lynx brand as 'about as fashionable as Roger Moore in a safari suit'.

Its 'Lynx Effect' re-positioning made it the premier 'aid to seduction' for a generation of mid- to late-teen males. By the early 2000s it had a 19% share of the UK male toiletries market and was used by 50% of all 11–24-year-old males at least once a week (Source: Guardian Media Section). Autopilot status amongst its target customers was firmly secured; as a consequence, growth baked in for the Lynx brand.

Autopilot example: Premier Inn

Another brand that drove significant growth by repositioning to secure autopilot status is Premier Inn, following its 'wake up wonderful' campaign fronted by advertisements that featured Lenny Henry.

By understanding that budget travellers value a good night's sleep above everything else, and re-positioning itself to 'own' this attribute via its superior mattresses and pillows, its 'Good Night' Guarantee and the Lenny Henry campaign, Premier Inn broke out of the budget hotel pack and secured autopilot status for budget travellers – in particular for businessmen staying away from home.

Autopilot status secured, the brand now has an almost 40% share of the budget hotel category and has outgrown its competitors in each of the last five years.

Autopilot example: Uber

Uber is a little different from the two examples above. Rather than an established but undifferentiated brand which repositioned itself to become the default choice in a crowded category, Uber came from nowhere to establish itself as the autopilot choice by offering a proposition totally unlike established taxi-hire companies.

For reasons explained later in this chapter, Uber's proposition connected emotionally with its target consumers in a way traditional taxis could not match; it became the unchallenged autopilot choice for young, busy urban professionals in every city in which it launched. From a standing start when it launched in San Francisco in 2011, Uber is today valued at over US$60bn and operates in 58 countries and over 300 cities. It is a compelling example of what can be achieved when autopilot status for a key group of customers is secured.

What's so interesting about each of these cases is that it was propositional change that drove these sudden inflexion points in the growth trends of these brands. Pricing, promotions and marketing strategy all stayed pretty much consistent with the 'pre-growth' period (or, in the case of Uber, were simply not an issue): it was what these brands were promising and how they delivered it which changed – and the results were pretty spectacular.

This gives a clue as to how autopilot status can be attained. We'll come back to some of these brands, and in particular the propositional changes that made such a difference for them, later in this chapter. In the meantime, how do brands get to become the autopilot choice for significant groups of consumers? When are autopilot decisions taken, what drives them and how can we influence them?

Well, it's tough. The biggest reason that it's tough to understand how and why autopilot decisions are taken is that, mostly, we make these decisions subconsciously – in effect, we're not aware that we are making them.

In Chapter 1, I used the example of a default TV channel choice to illustrate how we all operate on 'autopilot' in most of our everyday decisions. Think of your own autopilot TV channels. Think about when you made these decisions and why you decided to make these particular channels your default favourites (or autopilots).

Your autopilot TV channels are (insert answers here):

You decided to make these channels your autopilot on the following occasions (try to be as exact with the date and time of these choices as possible):

Finally, the reason you decided to choose these as your autopilots was (again, what was the one key reason that each of these channels got your autopilot vote):

What? Finding it difficult? Can't remember exactly when you decided to default to these channels? Equally hard to recall what it was that made you decide to make these autopilot choices? That's because these decisions will have been taken subconsciously.

In a way, that seems strange. Decisions that have quite a big impact in our daily lives being taken without us doing so consciously doesn't feel quite right. In fact, subconscious decision making of this sort makes absolute sense.

Daniel Kahneman won the Nobel Prize in 2002 for his ground-breaking work in understanding how our brains operate, particularly how we make the many thousands of daily decisions with which we run our lives. The essence of Kahneman's brilliant work was to identify that our brains have two modes of operation: 'System 1', which operates subconsciously and whose operation we are unaware of; and 'System 2', our conscious thought processes which we are fully aware of and which constitute most of what we believe our brains spend their time doing.

In fact, we couldn't be more wrong.

Our subconscious System 1 operates incredibly fast, can process huge amounts of information virtually instantaneously, works almost effortlessly and is responsible for around 90–95% of all the decisions we make each day. Without the incredible processing speed and efficiency of System 1, we would not be able to get much beyond weighing up the pros and cons of which breakfast cereal to eat, exactly how much milk to pour on top and whether the taste benefits of adding sugar will be outweighed by its negative health impacts (I may exaggerate a little here for effect . . .).

Our System 2 conscious brain works much more slowly. System 2 is used when we encounter new situations where our automatic System 1 brains have not got enough background data to decide automatically what we should do. System 2 considers new data carefully, weighs it against positive or negative outcomes, searches our experience for useful parallels, and then, slowly, makes a decision. In new situations or when we consciously decide we want to make a change from the way we usually do things, System 2 is essential. For the vast majority of our everyday decisions, System 2 doesn't come into it – System 1 has decided for us before we are even aware we are making the decisions.

This is how our subconscious autopilot decision making works.

This behaviour goes on in every area of our lives – and it's a very good job it does. Were there to be no subconscious System 1 operating we would be condemned to a constant re-evaluation of all viable alternatives in all areas of our lives – and that, as you can imagine, would make it pretty difficult to get much done. In the vast majority of cases it is System 1 that is making our autopilot decisions – which explains why we are aware of so few of them.

Since Kahneman published his work, many academics and behavioural scientists have studied and commented on this phenomenon. Here are a couple of the more pertinent observations:

> System 1 and System 2 are both active whenever we are awake ... System 2 normally in a low-effort mode. System 1 continuously generates suggestions for System 2 ... (and) when all goes smoothly, which is most of the time, System 2 adopts the suggestions of System 1 with little or no modification.
>
> Kahneman (2011)

> The most important part of any buyer's purchasing process occurs almost entirely without being noticed ... buyers in effect 'decide' not to consider the vast majority of brands in the market. Instead, they notice a few, and quite often, only one.
>
> Sharp (2010)

The Growth Director says:

Autopilot decisions are taken subconsciously . . . we're rarely aware that we have taken them.

- Autopilot decisions are taken mostly subconsciously by our super-fast, almost effortless System 1 decision-making processes.

- System 1 is our subconscious brain. It is super-fast, can process huge amounts of data, works almost effortlessly, and guides around 95% of all the decisions we make each day.
- System 2 is the conscious part of our brain that we are aware of. Compared to System 1, it is slow and can only handle limited amounts of data. System 2 is used to evaluate new or significantly changed situations where more thoughtful consideration is needed.
- Autopilot decisions are driven as much by emotional factors as by rational ones; we are usually not consciously aware that we have made an 'autopilot' choice – it's System 1 at work.

For now, that's all I'm going to say about System 1 and System 2. Chapter 4 of this book provides more detail on the brain science behind the brand choices we make – and, if you really want to go to the source of all this thinking, then buy Daniel Kahneman's *Thinking Fast and Slow*.

So if autopilot decisions are made mostly subconsciously, does this mean that there's nothing we can do to understand or influence them? Well, fortunately, no.

The first aspect of autopilot choice that we need to understand is 'when' these decisions are made. Luckily, we know a bit about this. The first point to re-stress is that we choose products to meet higher-level emotional goals. Each time we make a purchase we have to give away something that we value – money –so our subconscious brains are constantly trying to maximise the compensating value that we derive from the purchase by choosing a brand that will enable us to fulfill the most important emotional goal driving us in any given situation.

The better a brand is perceived to fit with the dominant emotional goal that we are pursuing, the greater its value to us and thus the bigger 'win' its purchase represents.

This leads to what Phil Barden describes as 'The Winner Takes All Effect':

> Consumers choose the product with the highest fit to their dominant emotional goal in a given situation.
>
> Barden (2013)

Our subconscious brains are always intuitively aware of the emotional goals relevant to any given situation, and will adjust to focus against the dominant goal in any set of circumstances. So a desire for a mid-morning snack might lead a consumer to choose a chocolate bar if the dominant goal involved getting a fast energy boost, while the same consumer might choose an apple or a bag of nuts if circumstances meant that finding a healthier snack had become more dominant. A car buyer needs a car to travel from one destination to another, but would choose a brand like Volvo if safety was the dominant goal or Mercedes if speed and status were more important. The Volvo buyer would probably not even consider Mercedes as an alternative (not ranked in the 'safety' consideration set) and vice-versa for the Mercedes buyer.

How do we (subconsciously) decide which of the many competing brands in a category – often offering broadly similar performance promises – is the one that will best enable us to achieve our dominant emotional goal?

This is where context becomes all-important to our subconscious brains. Context significantly changes the way we think about things. Here's a simplistic example of the difference that context makes to our perceptions. Take a look at the two small squares in the diagram below. You will see them as different shades of grey, but they are exactly the same colour. The reason that you see them as different is because of the background colour behind them. This contextual difference makes our brains see the colours as being different when they are, in fact, identical.

Figure 3.1

While this visual example of the impact of context is rather simplistic, it makes the point about how our brains function when they are making decisions. The context relevant at that point is not a background colour, but rather the situations in which our brains have experienced, or can imagine experiencing, using the product we are about to choose.

Because of their huge data-processing ability, our System 1 brains are able to remember all the relevant situations we have experienced in the past and can imagine the range of situations we are likely to encounter in the future. Thus, when we are facing a choice between brands that offer broadly similar performance attributes, our System 1 brains will imagine the situation where attainment of the relevant dominant emotional goal is most important to us or most difficult for us to achieve, and will select the brand that it thinks will best enable us to meet our goals even in this 'maximum stress' situation.

Once a brand has been selected as the best available for this moment of maximum emotional importance, System 1 will default to it every time it is required to make a purchase decision in this category. This helps explain why, even in a category like cars where frequency of purchase is very low, over 50% of new cars are the same brand that the owner chose last time. Unless their emotional goals while driving have changed, they would be most unlikely to change their preferred brand.

To summarise: autopilot choices are made at a small number of key usage moments when the performance of the product or service has a disproportionate *emotional* impact on the user. We call these 'Moments of Maximum Emotional Impact' (or MoMIs).

Let's look a little more closely at how MoMIs influence autopilot choice.

Rather than an infrequent, high-value purchase category like cars, let's look at the other end of the spectrum – a functional, frequently purchased item such as deodorant.

The starting point, of course, is to remember that, even in this category, all the products we ever buy are driven by a set of emotional goals that we are trying to fulfil. I don't think I'm speculating too much to assert that no-one has ever woken up in the morning thinking 'I know what I'm going to do today . . . buy a can of deodorant!' – However, lots of people will have woken up and thought 'I'm meeting that really important/attractive person for lunch today . . . better make sure I look and feel my best'. That desire to go to lunch feeling confident and secure may well drive them to go out and buy a deodorant.

This holds true for the motivations behind most of what we do in our daily lives – and for the reasons we purchase pretty much all of the consumer products and services that we use.

To illustrate further – and still sticking with deodorants (sorry . . .). If you are a middle-aged businessman, then perhaps the biggest emotional driver for your usage of deodorants might be to be confident that you would stay dry and protected from odour throughout a long working day . . . even in a highly stressful moment (MoMI) such as sitting next to the boss in a meeting at the end of the day. Based upon that set of emotional needs, it's likely that your subconscious autopilot choice would be a product/brand that had convinced you it delivered long-lasting dryness . . . for example, 'Sure'.

But, if you were a mid- to late-teenage boy, your emotional driver is likely to be very different. You probably would not care about whether your deodorant would still be working when you were out meeting with your mates in eight hours' time . . . but you might be incredibly emotionally motivated to choose a deodorant that might just enhance your attractiveness if you were likely to be in a situation where you might encounter girls. This might lead your subconscious to choose a brand like . . . say . . . 'Lynx'.

As our System 1 brains are hard-wired to search for and notice brands that deliver the emotional benefits that we need, each of these two very different consumers would subconsciously notice the brands that 'ticked the right emotional goal boxes' and would find themselves defaulting to purchase these brands, probably without ever realising they were making this conscious decision.

It's important here to notice the difference between the broad 'emotional goal states' we are trying to satisfy and the MoMIs when these emotions are at their height.

Satisfying broad emotional needs is fine for a brand and is likely to lead to some commercial success. However, the brands that our subconscious brains will be most drawn to choose as our autopilots will be those that show they understand those super-powerful moments when emotional need states are at their height, and have developed products/services/ marketing campaigns focusing on these. These brands are the real autopilot winners.

To illustrate, let's go back to two clear autopilot winners: Lynx deodorant/body spray, and the Uber taxi company. These are both great examples of brands that have had striking success (whether by accident or design) by understanding the key moments when their target customers were most emotionally engaged with their product, and then developing and executing propositions that were significantly better than all their competitors at satisfying the needs that were at their height at these moments.

Lynx

Lynx (also called Axe in some countries) is a range of deodorants/ bodysprays produced and marketed by Unilever. Its core customer is a young male – with a particular skew towards mid/late teenage boys. The deodorant/bodyspray market is mainly skewed towards the needs of adults: many brands are targeted at women and emphasise femininity, skin sensitivity, gentle protection, etc. Another group of brands is targeted more towards older males and emphasises strength, dryness, long-lasting deodorant effect, etc.

None of these emotional goals are particularly relevant to teenage boys.

However, there is one situation in which this group suddenly becomes super-engaged with their personal hygiene. This is, of course, when they are in the proximity of girls. At this time (and, perhaps for some, only at this time), they very much want their deodorant to be working. More than that, they would very much like it if whatever it was that their deodorant used as a fragrance proved to enhance their attractiveness to the opposite sex. Of all the many usage situations this group ever found themselves in, there was just one MoMI – that when young boys found themselves confronted by young girls.

Lynx understood this MoMI and crafted their whole brand proposition around it. They designed packaging that looked strong, masculine and dynamic, with bold, strong colours and a steamlined can shape. They used strong and slightly exotic fragrances designed to effectively cut through, or mask, the ... er ... underlying natural fragrance of their target consumer!

Crucially, they developed a marketing and advertising approach that, with maximum impact, activated the emotions behind that crucial MoMI. The tag-line 'Spray More ... Get More', together with tongue-in-cheek advertising campaigns featuring hyper-normal young guys attracting 'out of their league' girls, has to be one of the most direct (and commercially effective) lines ever developed.

Of course, this highly targeted approach that enabled Lynx/Axe to own this key MoMI was hugely successful in making Lynx/Axe the dominant autopilot choice for its chosen demographic – mid-late teenage males.

This is a wonderful illustration of how owning the key MoMI will inevitably deliver autopilot status ... and growth. Recall from earlier in this chapter how this brilliant re-positioning took Lynx from being a small, stagnant brand in the mid-1990s, to a brand with around 19% of the male toiletries market just ten years later – a brand used by 50% of 11–24-year-old males at least once each week.

A brand with a very different target consumer, a very different commercial approach ... but equal autopilot success is Uber, the smartphone-enabled taxi hire company.

Uber

Again, Uber understood the emotional components behind finding a taxi. Usually, when we need to get a taxi, we need to get somewhere fast – or we wouldn't bother with the expense. Perhaps we are en route to or from an important meeting; perhaps wanting to get home quickly after working late; or needing to get home after a night out.

In all these cases our concerns are not really about whether we will eventually get a taxi – it's about how long it will take us to find one/how difficult the process of finding it will be. We also fear being 'ripped off' by drivers taking advantage of our reliance on them – and in some cases being driven in decrepit, unsafe cars.

For Uber, that MoMI is when you realise you need to find a taxi . . . and immediately your heart sinks at the prospect.

The Uber proposition brilliantly resolves this. By utilising the smartphone technology that almost all its target customers will have, Uber enables its subscribers to be completely confident that they will be able to call a taxi when they want one, they will know exactly how long it will take to get to them and they will have a good idea of what the cost will be.

Even if it would have been quicker to hail a cab in the street, the Uber proposition hands control of the process to the customer in a way that taking your chances in the street or asking someone to call a local car hire firm ('we'll be with you in about 20 minutes . . . or might be a little longer . . .') just cannot match. Control – or lack of it – is the emotional button that Uber is pressing; this proposition plays brilliantly to those MoMIs when being sure that a taxi is on its way is of high importance to you.

The Growth Director says:

Owning emotionally important 'Moments of Maximum Emotional Impact' (or MoMIs) is the key to becoming the autopilot choice of your target customers.

- Autopilot decisions are driven by a small number of key usage moments – MoMIs – when the performance of a product/service is of disproportionate emotional importance to us.
- Owning the broad emotional territory is powerful . . . owning the moment when those emotions are at their height is much more powerful and is what drives the most successful autopilot brands.
- Brands that identify these MoMIs and develop/bring to market propositions that satisfy the emotional needs behind these moments will become the default autopilot choice for the group of consumers for whom the identified MoMIs are most important.
- In most cases, identifying and understanding the emotions behind these moments is not easy . . . the subconscious brain is driving these decisions and we do not easily have access to it.

Case Study: Stella Artois: Building Propositions Around Moments of Maximum Emotional Impact; *by Stef Calcraft, Founding Partner, Mother Advertising Agency*

In his years running the Mother Advertising Agency, Stef came across a number of brands who had identified the 'Moments of Maximum Emotional Impact' and making these the focus of their propositional and marketing efforts.

One powerful example of this is the work that Stef and Mother did on the Stella Artois brand.

'One example I experienced of the power of owning the emotionally important moment was when we took over advertising for the Stella Artois brand.

We saw quickly that, in order to grow, we needed to differentiate Stella from the many mass market, 'blokey' lagers on the market. To do this we wanted to take the brand back to its French heritage and to emphasise its high quality, slightly exotic equity.

We recognised fairly quickly that, for the young male drinkers we were targeting, the key 'moment' when brand choice is most emotionally important is when the drink is ordered at the bar. Your choice of brand in this social situation, often with friends or potentially attractive strangers around, is the moment when you care most about choosing the 'right' brand.

So the challenge was to work out how to own this moment in a way that was attractive, distinctive and essentially 'Stella'.

The first step towards doing this was to create a Stella 'brand world' that evoked an uber-stylised 1960s French Riviera where the effortlessly cool French guys and the equally effortlessly stylish French women all drank Stella. This instantly gave us creative distinctivitness compared to all the competitive beer brands and drove the development of some great TV ads and some massively impactful (and very beautiful) poster work.

This highly distinctive 'brand world' gave us the ability to stand out from other brands and thus the potential to grab ownership of that key emotionally important moment. But how could we evoke this stylish, super-cool, essentially French world in the middle of bars in pubs and clubs all over Great Britain?

Our client helped us find the answers to this challenge. There were two particularly important elements:

The first was an emphasis on the beautiful, and unusual, 'chalice' glass that we used in all our ads, and in which the company encouraged Stella to be served wherever possible. This stylish, distinctive glass – and the elegant glass bottles in which Stella is sold – immediately communicated its different equity – drinking from the chalice while your friends were glugging other beers from conventional pint glasses immediately set Stella apart and evoked its stylish French equity.

This wasn't an especially easy decision for the Stella company to make. The chalice glass held less than conventional glasses, so emphasising its use could have been seen as a risk to volume. But because the Stella team understood the power of differentiating themselves at this key moment they were prepared to take the risk – and it paid off.

Secondly, the client identified an unusual (and unique) pouring ritual that the brand taught bartenders – a '9-Step' process which, by requiring the customer to wait a little while the beer was poured, allowed to settle, cleared of excess foam, topped up, and then served, emphasised both the quality of the beer and the mature patience of those who had the discernment to drink it.

Isn't that a powerful message to be sending to your friends as you are all standing at the bar together?

This ritual became such an important way to communicate the distinctiveness and perceived superiority of the brand that we often featured it in our advertisements.

Together, these elements allowed Stella to differentiate itself positively from all other beers at that crucial moment at the bar – and suddenly made it a much more desirable 'autopilot' choice for the young aspirational male drinkers we were targeting.'

Stella is a great example of how the best brands bring their proposition to life and capture the key 'Moments of Maximum Emotional Impact' through all elements of their commercial plan – product, packaging, service, distribution channels – even pricing. It's very hard to truly own those key 'moments' with advertising alone – your brand has to deliver as well. Moments are real – and very powerful. Understand, and own them for your brand, and you are on the way to profitable growth.

The Growth Director's Summary

- The key to Good Growth is becoming the default autopilot brand in your category . . . that's it.
- Our brains have hard-wired us to shop on autopilot from a small portfolio of favourite brands . . . most of the time we pay no attention to the efforts of other brands to secure our business
- Once secured, autopilot status delivers 75%+ of the purchases of your converted consumers and will 'recruit' more and more target customers month after month, year after year.
- Autopilot brands are likely to be much more profitable, as consumers will buy at full price and will stay loyal with much less marketing/promotional effort than other consumers.
- Autopilot decisions are taken mostly subconsciously by our super-fast, almost effortless System 1 decision-making processes – they are driven as much by emotional factors as by rational ones; we are usually not consciously aware that we have made an autopilot choice.
- Autopilot decisions are driven by a small number of key usage moments – Moments of Maximum Emotional Impact (MoMIs) when the performance of a product/service is of disproportionate emotional importance to us.
- Brands which identify these MoMIs and develop/bring to market propositions that satisfy the emotional needs behind these moments will become the default autopilot choice for the group of consumers for whom the identified MoMIs are most important. We looked at Lynx and Uber as two good examples of brands that have done this successfully.

Chapter 4

The Brain Science Behind Growth: How the way that our brains work determines which brands grow

Chapter 3 established that the key to sustained, significant, profitable 'Good Growth' is understanding how to become the default autopilot choice amongst your target shoppers. Autopilot brands, once chosen, get around 75% of our category purchases, we stay loyal to them and are happy to buy regularly even without promotional or price cutting incentives, and, because we connect emotionally with them we will advocate them to others – so generating a wonderful virtuous cycle of committed users recruiting more new users.

It further suggested that autopilot choices are made subconsciously by our System 1 brain processes at a small number of key 'Moments of Maximum Emotional Impact' (MoMIs) when the performance of the product/service we are choosing is disproportionately important to us.

Seems to make sense. But – is it true? Or, rather, are these conclusions (which have very radical implications for most businesses' commercial plans) based on good science? This chapter sets out to examine the evidence for the assertions we have made so far.

To begin, let's go back to 2002 when a super smart neuroscientist, Daniel Kahneman, won the Nobel Prize for his ground-breaking work into how our subconscious brains work and how they guide the vast majority of the decisions we make every day of our lives. While I'll summarise Kahneman's findings here, those who want to know more should buy *Thinking Fast and Slow* (2011), which lays out his work in much more detail than we have space for here (for the real science junkies his Nobel Prize winning paper is also available at www. nobelprize.org).

The essence of Kahneman's work, at least as far as its implications for the contents of this book go, is probably best summarised as follows:

> Our brain is not made for thinking, but for fast and automated actions.

This powerful and challenging summary is not, unfortunately, mine, but belongs to Phil Barden's book *Decoded* (2013) which does a fantastic job of explaining the implications of Kahneman's work for the way our brands are perceived and our purchase decisions made. So what was it in Kahneman's work which led Barden to this pithy conclusion?

The core breakthrough in Kahneman's work is that it identifies two separate thinking and decision-making systems within our brains:

- *System 1* integrates perception and intuition. It's super-fast, runs continuously, can effortlessly handle huge amounts of data and drives around 90–95% of all the decisions we ever make. System 1 works subconsciously and we are not aware of it operating.
- *System 2* is our conscious, evaluatory, thinking process. It is slow, effortful and can only cope with limited amounts of data. It accounts for around 5–10% of the decisions we make and is what we regard as us 'thinking'.

The two key points here are: (i) the conscious, evaluatory (System 2) processes that we are aware of and regard as us 'thinking' account for only 5– 10% of the decisions we make and (ii) the System 1 processes that account for 90–95% of all the decisions we make are subconscious and we are simply not aware of them. These two points have huge implications for the way we need to go about understanding our shopping behaviour and choice of brands, and therefore for the way we should set about developing strategies and plans to enable our brands, and our businesses, to grow. In particular they help us to understand why the phenomenon of autopilot shopping exists, and why it is such a dominant force in our choice of brands and our loyalty to them.

Let's examine System 1 and System 2 and their implications for our lives (and our shopping behaviour) a little more closely. The first point to make is that without our super-fast, super-efficient System 1 processes, we simply could not cope with the complexity of our daily lives. Our System 2 processes are not only slow, but require significant amounts of effort for even simple pieces of considered, evaluatory, thinking.

As a simple example of this is – the next time you are out walking with someone, ask them to complete a relatively simple multiplication task: say, 12 x 76, and ask them to give you the answer immediately. If they make a serious attempt to provide you with an immediate answer, they will stop walking and stand still while making the calculation. It is simply too difficult, and too much effort for them to engage their System 2 brains in completing this relatively simple task while simultaneously staying focused on their direction of travel, hazards along the way etc. The saying 'he can't walk and chew gum at the same time' is probably not too far away from being genuinely illustrative of the difficulty our conscious brains have in engaging on more than one task at a time.

Another simple and very effective demonstration of the slow, effortful way in which our conscious brains work is the well-known 'Stroop Effect' exercise which has been used as an illustrative example by Daniel Kahneman, amongst others. This presents the brain with the simple task of distinguishing between the colour of a word and the colour in which it is printed. It's a great way to understand just how ponderous our conscious brains can be with even very simple tasks – if you'd like to take the test (it only takes around 60 seconds) then search 'Interactive Stroop Effect Experiment' online.

These two simple examples illustrate nicely how engaging our System 2 conscious brains is slow, difficult and effortful. If we engaged System 2 every time we had a decision to make we would very swiftly become overloaded with the effort and would get almost nothing done. Just imagine how difficult it would be to navigate the incredible complexity of choice presented to you in a typical supermarket using your slow, evaluatory, System 2 brain. As a result we learn to avoid engaging System 2 whenever we can, and try to operate as much as possible using our super-fast, super-efficient, effortless but subconscious System 1 brains.

Kahneman sums this up nicely. He says:

We find cognitive effort at least mildly unpleasant and avoid it as much as possible.

Kahneman (2011)

What, then, are the implications of this effort-averse behaviour when it comes to brand choice and shopping decisions?

Well, when we encounter a new type of product for the first time (e.g. when the first lap-top computers came along) we have no 'historical' data for our System 1 brains to guide us with, so have no choice but to engage System 2 to understand what the new products do, how alternatives differ from each other, whether or not they might be suitable for us and whether we should buy them. This takes time and effort; we will find ourselves scanning comparative data online, reading reviews of products in our newspapers, asking advice from knowledgeable friends etc.

Pretty soon, though, we have internalised these evaluations, will have decided whether to make an initial purchase or not and will have started to build a history of usage. Soon, it is simply too much trouble and effort to continue these evaluations consciously – we need to free up our System 2 brains to move onto something else. So, without realising it, we 'sub-contract' decision-making to our subconscious and let System 1 take over.

System 1 goes to work by feeding in details of every new usage/purchase experience, noticing and remembering new reviews we might have read, filing away comments from friends etc and will use all these inputs to suggest purchase decisions to System 2. In the vast majority of cases, because we do not want to engage System 2 unless we really have to, the System 1 suggestions are endorsed, and we follow the brand choices and purchase decisions that our sub-conscious brains recommend without ever consciously 'thinking about them'.

This, then, is Important Science Point 1: Due to the slow and effortful nature of our conscious (System 2) brains we quickly pass decision making on the brands we buy to our System 1 brains and we make most of our subsequent purchase decisions subconsciously.

Now that's all very well. If we've accepted that our subconscious System 1 brains guide most of our purchasing behaviour, then on what basis is System 1 making its decisions? Well, this comes down to understanding our motivations for buying products and services of any sort. Obviously, the very act of buying a product or service involves us giving away something that we value very highly – money. It stands to reason that we would not do this unless we felt that the thing we were getting in exchange was worth the trade. Why are we willing to so readily trade a commodity (money) that we value so highly for products with as little intrinsic interest and value to us as, say, nuts and bolts, washing powder, or deodorants?

Well, of course it's not the products themselves we want, it's what they will enable us to do. Or, more accurately, which goals they will enable us to meet. The famous Harvard Professor Dr Theodore Levitt said it best: 'People don't want to buy a quarter-inch drill – they want a quarter-inch hole.' Cited in Clayton Christensen (2016), *The Clayton Christensen Reader*, p. 46.

Such insights give us the clue to understanding how our autopilot choices are made – identifying and understanding the goals that our subconscious brains are seeking to help us to meet by choosing to purchase products from a particular category, and then to choose brand X over brand Y.

So what do I mean when I talk about these 'goals'? Well, that brings us to *Important Science Point 2*:

Work by many neuroscientists, anthropologists and behavioural economists have identified that ALL our activities are driven by seeking to meet some combination of deep-rooted motivational goals. These existed long before products and brands were invented and our compulsion to meet them is hard-wired deep in our subconscious and emotional selves.

The Growth Director says:

We choose brands subconsciously by fitting them to our most important motivational goals.

- Remember Phil Barden's great quote: 'our brains are not made for thinking but for fast and automated actions'.
- Our subconscious 'System 1' brains are super-efficient and take 90–95% of all the decisions we ever make.

- In order to cope with the complexity of our lives the vast majority of purchase decisions and brand choices are taken subconsciously by our System 1 brains.
- Purchase decisions are driven by a desire to satisfy some combination of deep-rooted motivational goals.
- Brand choices are made by our System 1 brains finding the best fit between the available brands and the dominant motivational goals we are trying to satisfy.

The best and most manageable summary of these goals which I have found (and again I make no apologies for borrowing – with permission! – from Barden and his company, Decode Marketing) is to describe the six main goals as follows:

- *Security*: the need for care, trust, closeness, security and warmth.
- *Enjoyment*: the need for relaxation, light heartedness and pleasure.
- *Excitement*: the need for vitality, fun, creativity and new experiences.
- *Adventure*: the need for freedom, courage, rebellion and risk.
- *Autonomy*: the need for success, power, recognition and superiority.
- *Discipline*: the need for precision, order, logic and certainty.

All human activity can be described as striving to meet some combination of these motivational goals in any situation in which we find ourselves. All product purchases are driven by the extent to which we believe our product choice will enable us to meet the relevant goals. This phenomenon has been noted and commented on by behavioural scientists for many years:

> If you understand the goals your consumers are pursuing, and connect your product to the satisfaction of those goals, your consumers will find a way to get to your products.
>
> Genco et al (2013)

In the context of consumer products and services it is true to say that in almost all cases meeting the relevant goals will require a product/service to 'perform' on two levels: an explicit, functional level (like getting clothes clean or providing food which is both nutritious and tastes good) and an implicit, emotional level (like sending signals about the type of mother you are through your detergent choice, or seeking variety or an unusual taste experience via the 'exotic' ready meals you buy).

All categories will have a set of basic explicit goals that all products must meet if they are to be purchased (e.g. for a detergent product that would be cleaning efficacy, acceptable perfume, packaging that is easy to use etc). Typically, the market leader will 'own' these goals in consumers' minds, and any perceived weaknesses in these areas by other brands will severely restrict their attractiveness. However, and crucially, in most mature consumer markets, all competing products perform to broadly equivalent levels on the explicit goals, making brand differentiation on this basis very difficult.

Remember – effective differentiation means being not only technically better (being able to show in a lab environment that your detergent washes 5% whiter than others) but being better in a way which is meaningful and valued by consumers. In markets where all products provide very acceptable levels of performance (and most mature consumer markets have reached this stage – the brands that failed to do this will have dropped out) trying to differentiate your brand by promising a little bit more performance is very hard – and will probably be ineffective.

Yet many consumer companies continue to pursue commercial strategies that are based on trying to differentiate themselves in this way. Think about the number of car companies trying to persuade consumers that an extra 5% brake horsepower/acceleration time 0–60mph/fuel efficiency/reduction in CO_2 emissions makes a meaningful difference ... or the supermarkets shouting about how their particular mix of price cuts and promotions represent better value than the virtually identical set offered by their competitors ... or the banks tweaking savings rates up and down within a quarter of a point of each other (and promising almost identical levels of considerate, personalised service).

All technical differentiators, of course ... but meaningful for consumers? Often, they are not ...

While there are, of course, circumstances in which meaningful differentiation based on explicit, functional performance is possible (and later chapters will examine some of these), the key to effective brand differentiation is much more likely to lie in understanding how to 'own' the dominant implicit emotional goal for the consumers you wish to target. If you are able to do this, then you will become the autopilot choice for the consumers for whom this goal is the dominant driving force – even if you are not differentiated from other brands in a functional explicit sense.

To illustrate this, let's go back to the example I used earlier from the deodorant category. For most consumers in this category the dominant goals will be associated with territories like discipline (being certain you will stay dry all day), with perhaps some elements of security (care, trust) for women and perhaps some of autonomy (signals of power, success) for men.

For one sub-group of consumers, though, the dominant goal is very different. For young males, and probably only for this group, the dominant goal in using deodorants is to enhance their attractiveness to females – that's probably a combination of excitement and enjoyment goals. In the context of this category and this group of consumers the best way to describe this goal is probably 'seduction'. Lynx/Axe has understood this superbly, and has crafted a proposition that is targeted single-mindedly against persuading this specific consumer group that purchase of their products will enhance their chances of a successful seduction.

For all other consumers in the category this goal is not relevant to the product category of deodorants, so the proposition has very specific appeal. However, because the consumer sub-group is large enough, and because Lynx/Axe has been able to completely 'own' this goal territory, the brand has become hugely successful – even against very strong competitors like Sure, Gillette etc.

Notably, Lynx/Axe makes no attempt to persuade consumers that it is better than its competitors on the category's explicit goals of dryness, being long-lasting, kindness to skin, fragrance etc. It has focused solely on 'owning' the relevant implict goal (although it performs perfectly adequately in a functional sense) and has hence been able to differentiate itself very effectively – and to grow significantly in this highly competitive market.

One further very important point on goal territories. The dominant goal for us may change from purchase occasion to purchase occasion depending on the context in which we intend to use the product or service or the prevailing circumstances in our lives.

So – to take a simple illustrative example – let's think about purchasing a chocolate product. If our dominant goal motivation at the time of purchase is to buy a product to reward or indulge ourselves we might choose an expensive box of chocolates or a high-quality bar; if we are about to go into a social situation where sharing with others has high value then we might buy a box of Cadbury's 'Roses' or equivalent; if we are buying a product to keep us going between breakfast and lunch we might buy a brand with 'high energy' connotations like Snickers or, of course, Mars. We might even, if we were expecting to entertain friends with high moral principles, choose a Fairtrade product to signal our own similar beliefs and values.

The point is that as our goal motivations change, so too might our choice of brand – and this illustrates the danger of targeting consumers by simple socio-demographics. Depending upon the context created by our changing circumstances, our motivations are likely to change quite frequently – meaning that it is essential to target goal territories rather than an overly simplified demographic. We'll come back to this very important targeting point in later chapters.

We have established two very important, but quite hard to reconcile points.

- *Point 1*: Purchases of products and services are driven by the extent to which we believe those products/services will help us to meet whatever the dominant emotional goals are for us in a given situation.
- *Point 2*: The vast majority of the purchase decisions that we take are taken sub-consciously by our System 1 brains.

How do these two points fit together? Well, again it comes down to how our brains have evolved to cope with the massive complexity of our lives. If we were constantly having to consciously compare and evaluate brand choices within a category against the mix of implict/explicit goals that we were pursuing in buying into that category then we would never get much further than one or two decisions a day – and our

System 2 conscious brains would overload very quickly indeed! So, of course, our super-efficient System 1 brains take over.

As we travel around a supermarket (to take one particularly stressed example of product choice) we need to be simultaneously considering and evaluating a huge range of variable information. First, we would need to remember the various goals we are trying to satisfy on this shopping trip (fast, cheap meal to prepare for the kids; dinner party with work colleagues on Friday; romantic night in with partner; budget constraints etc). We would then need to recall all the accumulated experience we have had with different products/brands, the advertising messages we have recently seen, the recommendations of friends etc; finally, we need to be aware of relevant new information available in the supermarket itself – promotions, new products, special offers etc.

As we established earlier, this would represent huge information overload for our conscious brains, and we would find decision-making on this scale close to impossible. Our subconscious System 1 brains, however, can cope with this complexity in an instant. Without realising we are doing it, our System 1 brain will remember all the goals we are shopping for, will: notice the categories and brands with potential to meet those goals; recall all the experience we have had with those brands plus the advertisements we have seen; and notice and evaluate offers and other relevant activity in the supermarket itself.

Without us being aware of the process, System 1 will evaluate all this information and will prompt us to make the best available brand choice. The key to this incredible speed of choice is that our System 1 brain knows the basis upon which we are choosing – that is finding the brand that best enables us to meet our dominant motivational goal – and so is able to come to an instantaneous purchase recommendation without any need to engage our slow, evaluatory System 2 brain. This is how we are able to make dozens of sophisticated product purchase decisions virtually instantaneously as we walk through those incredibly crowded supermarket aisles.

This truth has huge consequences for wasted effort in sales/marketing programmes – and is something we'll return to in some detail later in this book. What all this shows us is that purchase decisions are driven by finding the brand that fits best with the dominant goal in any given situation – and our subconscious brain only notices (perhaps 'pays attention to' would be a better description) the brand that it has decided provides the best fit and directs us to choose it without any detailed evaluation of alternatives.

That's fine as far as it goes – but it doesn't yet quite explain the phenomenon of autopilot brands and our extreme loyalty to them once chosen. This brings us to *Important Science Point 3*.

The autopilot phenomenon is best explained by the speed and complexity at which our subconscious brains process the data with which we make brand choice decisions. At some point when we start using a category we will decide (often subconsciously) that brand A is the best available to meet the particular mix of implicit and explicit goals that we are seeking to fulfill. As we start using brand A, the associations in our subconscious brains between it and the desired goal outcome will become reinforced by satisfactory usage of the product, by our subconscious brain 'noticing' reinforcing messages about brand A (in its packaging, advertising, comments from friends etc) and by it screening out messages from competing brands that it has decided do not enable us to meet our goals so well. This reinforcement cycle will become stronger as time goes on – so the more we choose, use and are satisfied with our autopilot brand, the less likely we will be to notice or pay attention to competing brands; the more we will notice and will value the marketing messages our autopilot is putting out and so the more its autopilot status will be reinforced with our controlling System 1 brains.

This reinforcement cycle illustrates the difficulty (indeed often the futility) of new brands attempting to compete with established market leaders on their own terms (i.e. by trying to persuade consumers that they provide what the market leading brand does . . . but a little better). For this approach to be successful, the challenger brands needs to be able to overcome all those years of autopilot reinforcement which have convinced users' System 1 brains that choosing the market leader is a very smart choice. That's tough.

Once we have made a clear connection between a brand and satisfaction of an important goal, our subconscious System 1 brains are very reluctant to change their minds – even when quite compelling evidence that other, potentially better alternatives are available is presented. To illustrate this, try this simple exercise:

Take a look at the two lines below:

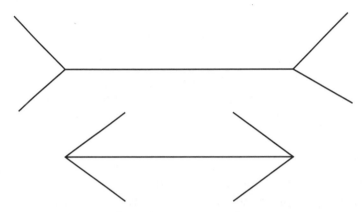

Figure 4.1 The Muller Lyer Illusion.

Which one is the longer? Easy isn't it? It's obviously the upper of the two lines.

Now, most of you, being sophisticated business types, will have seen this illusion before (it's called the Muller Lyer Illusion) and will be saying 'Look, we know the lines are the same length . . . we've seen this a million times. Why don't you show us something a bit more original?' Well, the illusion itself is not actually my point. My point is the way that your subconscious brain refuses to see the lines as equal – even when you know very well that they are. Even when we know this – even after measuring them to prove it – we find it almost impossible to 'see' them this way (go on – try it again now).

This reason we remain 'visually convinced' that the upper line is the longer is that, over time, our System 1 brains have learned that the 'visually open' cues given by the fins of the upper line are more usually associated with greater length than the 'visually closed' fins appended to the lower line. Because this is an impression hard-wired into our subconscious System 1 brains and reinforced many times over the years, we are very unwilling to change this perception even when our conscious System 2 is telling us 'we just measured the two lines and they are the same length!'.

This shows the enduring power of System 1 once it has made a decision – or for the purposes of this chapter, an autopilot brand choice. Put simply, our System 1 brains are very stubborn. Once chosen, it will take a lot of very persuasive evidence from other brands to get System 1 to switch its habitual choice. This brings us to a phenomenon which many business people will be familiar with – the difficulty for new/secondary brands to take a share from well-established market leaders.

The Growth Director says:

Emotions, not rational factors dominate brand choice.

- Motivational goals have two components – an explicit, functional component linked to performance and an implicit, emotional component linked to psychological goals.
- Differentiation via explicit goals is very difficult – all brands in a category tend to perform to similar levels and meaningful advantages are very hard to sustain.
- Usually, emotional drivers are much stronger than rational ones and therefore emotions, not performance differences, drive most of our brand choice decisions.
- Our sub-conscious 'System 1' brains are very efficient at spotting the best fit between the goals we are trying to achieve and the brand choices available.
- Once chosen, 'auto-pilot' brand preference becomes reinforced by repeated usage and is very hard to shift.

A brand which has established a leadership position in a market has done so by becoming the autopilot choice of the majority of consumers in that market. In turn, this will have been achieved by being chosen over all other competing brands as the one which best enables achievement of the dominant emotional goals driving category participation. As we have seen earlier in this chapter via the Muller Lyer Illusion, once the subconscious brains of the consumers participating in this category have made this choice, they will be very reluctant to change it – and indeed will seek reinforcement of this automatic purchase choice. Every time the leading brand is used (assuming it performs adequately), its choice is being reinforced with its users. Every time they view its advertising, their subconscious brain will receive further positive feedback that its autopilot decision was the right one.

Our subconscious brains raise the bar for challenger brands still higher by being actively resistant to advertising messages seeking to persuade it that it has made the wrong autopilot choice.

This is, of course, the way that our System 1 brains maintain confidence in the decisions we have made, and avoid having to engage slow, effortful System 2 to re-evaluate brand choices. From the point of view of helping us deal efficiently with the vast complexity of our lives these tendencies make a lot of sense – but if you are a secondary brand challenging a well-established incumbent it makes your task much, much harder.

There are many examples of the 'undeserved' strength that established market-leaders have which are explained by this System 1 preference for defending its autopilot choices. Perhaps one of the most powerful examples is in the soft drinks category between Coca Cola and Pepsi. Some years ago Pepsi attempted to attack Coke by emphasising its superior taste. After all, surely if it could demonstrate that its taste was significantly preferred to Coke then consumers would, logically, switch. Not so!

Although in blind taste tests (i.e. where the brand is not shown) Pepsi is consistently preferred to CocaCola by a ratio of around 70 to 30%, its brand share is significantly below that of Coke's in almost all markets around the world.

Coca-Cola	Pepsi	
30%	70%	Blind taste test preference
40–50%	10–15%	Typical market share ex US

No matter how much money Pepsi spent showing that its product won these blind tests time and again, it was unable to shift consumer preference. Simply, all those committed Coke drinkers were unwilling to be persuaded rationally that they had made the wrong autopilot choice and found ways to ignore the data presented to them or view it as irrelevant.

System 1 autopilot bias at work!

So – an important chapter. While this does not set out to be the book that provides a deep understanding of how our brains work, I hope there is enough here to explain reasonably clearly why the brand choice and purchase decision phenomena that the book describes are driven by the way our brains are hard-wired. The truth is that, most of the time we just can't help the brand choices we make!

However, understanding that most of our decision-making related to brand choice goes on subconsciously does set business people a real challenge. If we're not consciously aware of it how are we ever going to work out how to position our brands for growth? That's a huge challenge for the market research tools that the business world has been using for many years. I'm afraid to say that those 'conventional' research tools we are all familiar with: focus groups; one-on-one depth interviews; online/offline surveys; consumer panels, etc, are more likely to fail to meet this challenge than to succeed. That's a big problem.

To put it simply, almost all conventional research makes the assumption that we are rational beings able to explain the reasons behind past decisions and also able to articulate what factors might drive our decision making in the future. Based upon this assumption, conventional research has, over the years, developed a whole suite of commonly used tools that essentially ask people rational questions and accept their answers as likely to be both truthful and accurate.

Neuroscience has shown that this assumption is just plain wrong. As the preceding chapters have shown, around 90–95% of all the decisions we make are made subconsciously. Most of those decisions are driven by emotional factors than by rational ones and, when the two clash (as the Muller Lyer Illusion showed), our emotional convictions usually override our rational analyses. Conventional research cannot access our subconscious decision-making processes, and is also very poor at connecting with the emotions behind the decisions we make. As Genco and others put it:

> The dilemma for market researchers is obvious: emotions drive decisions – even explicit decisions – but we don't have conscious access to many of these emotional drivers. When researchers ask

people why they made a particular decision they query their memory and come up with a plausible answer, but that answer will most likely be wrong.

Genco et al (2013)

That's extremely concerning given the reliance most companies have placed on conventional research techniques to reveal consumer motivation and their decision-making criteria.

Surprisingly, this understanding of the limitations of conventional research techniques is not new. Way back in the late 1970s, Richard Nisbett and Timothy Wilson showed that, when asked what we think, we guess – and these guesses are no more accurate than if we are asked to speculate on what someone else is thinking! Worse still, Nisbett and Wilson's work showed that, even though it is often basically made up, we will be sincerely convinced that the explanations for behaviour that we are giving to market researchers are super-accurate descriptions of the truth. No wonder conventional research is prone to getting things wrong!

Maybe, though, this partly explains well-known phenomena like the oft-quoted stat that '80% of new product launches fail'. After all, if companies invest in extensive research for anything, it will be for the launch of new products – surely there has never been a new product launch that was not supported by strongly positive conventional research results? If 80% of those initiatives fail, doesn't that tell us something powerful but worrying about the accuracy of the research techniques we have all been using?

So, what to do? I'd endorse the recommendations of the team who put the *Neuromarketing for Dummies* book together:

(a) *Treat people's self-reports about why they made decisions with extreme caution.* They're probably rationalising their decisions, not explaining them.

(b) *Find and adopt measurement techniques that give you access to the non-conscious drivers of decisions.* This is the only way you'll have any chance of understanding why people actually make the decisions they make.

Hear, hear! But how . . .?

It is not the purpose of this book to describe in any detail the research techniques that have emerged over the last ten years from the world of neuroscience that are able to connect with our sub-conscious System 1 brains, understand the emotional goal drivers behind the decisions we make and identify the factors which most impact them. A range of such techniques and tools now exist, and are used to varying degrees by many of the leading research agencies – and by a growing number of smaller companies who specialise in neuroscience-based research. These tools range from laboratory-based techniques that directly monitor the brain's activity under different stimuli, to much more accessible tools that can run online/offline surveys linking speed of response to answers given to identify how and where our subconscious brains take over from our conscious ones (similar to the personality-profiling surveys many of you will be familiar with which use time pressure to connect with the sub-conscious brain). Some companies have also developed qualitative techniques that can access the subconscious brain's processes in a small group/one-on-one interview environment.

Without particularly advocating any specific set of tools I strongly recommend that your company investigates use of these techniques if you are seeking to understand and influence consumer decision making. For these purposes, the conventional tools you have probably been using for many years just do not work. The case study below from Phil Barden, whose company Decode Marketing is one of the leading practitioners of neuroscientific and 'Implicit' research techniques operating today, provides some further examples of the limitations of conventional research and how new tools based upon neuroscience can help.

I hope this chapter has provided a reasonable understanding of the brain science behind the decisions we make as consumers.

We now turn to how we can use this understanding to begin to build commercial and marketing plans that will secure autopilot status for your brands, and thus will deliver significant, sustained, profitable growth. The first area I want to turn to concerns targeting – how to identify the market sectors that provide your business with its best chance of such growth.

Phil Barden has spent his career in senior marketing positions at major consumer companies like Unilever, Diageo and T-Mobile. He discovered the power of neuroscience to provide insights unavailable to conventional research while working at T-Mobile, and was so impressed that he changed direction, immersed himself in the neuroscience field. He is now managing director of Decode Marketing, one of the leading global practitioners of neuropsychological research. Phil is the author of *Decoded* – in my view, the best book yet written on the way our brains work and affect our brand choices and purchasing behaviour.

Phil has done much work understanding how brands can connect with the goals that drive purchasing behaviour, and uses this Cadbury case study to illustrate how powerful it is when brands get this right – and how easily they can get things wrong!

Case Study: Cadbury's Dairy Milk Chocolate: How Matching Brands to Dominant Emotional Goals Drives Growth: And Why Conventional Research Doesn't Work; *by Phil Barden, Managing Director Decode Marketing*

'Most of you will remember the very impactful 'Gorilla' advertisement that Cadbury's ran for their Dairy Milk chocolate bar some years ago. The idea of using a gorilla to advertise a chocolate bar seems at first to be rather bizarre – but actually it was an inspired choice.

Cadbury's had understood that the dominant emotional goal when buying a product like Dairy Milk is around extreme personal enjoyment – 'indulgence' is probably the best description. We do not buy products like Dairy Milk for functional reasons like sustenance or balancing our diets – we buy them because we look forward to a wonderfully indulgent moment when we can reward ourselves by sitting down, often alone, and enjoying the sensation of sweet, creamy chocolate melting on our tongue.

Their task, then, was to produce an advertising campaign which evoked (and therefore came to 'own') this moment of anticipation and pure personal indulgence – and their 'Gorilla' ad did this, albeit in an unusual and highly exaggerated way.

'You'll probably recall the ad. The soundtrack is 'In the Air Tonight' – the well-known Phil Collins track. As the ad opens we hear this track, and gradually pull back to reveal a gorilla (!) sitting at a drumkit (!) and preparing himself for – something. He is on his own – signalling indulgent 'me time'. He appears to be listening to the music intently. He stretches his neck, flares his nostrils and flexes his shoulder muscles. He is waiting. The anticipation is palpable. Then, as the music builds to a climax he picks up the drumsticks and joins in ecstatically with the famous drum riff in the middle of the track. He throws back his head as if in ecstasy – a moment of pure indulgence.

Now, using a drum-playing gorilla to advertise chocolate is not a conventional or obvious choice – and yet the advertisement managed to capture the dominant emotions driving purchase of chocolate bars – extreme personal enjoyment, or indulgence. Neuroscientific research has captured the emotions that this advertisement triggered – the goal map that the ad produced is shown towards the end of this case study.

As you will see, despite its unconventional execution, the 'Gorilla' ad was very effective at triggering exactly the emotional goal combination of enjoyment and security (in the sense of safety, inclusion, warmth) that drive chocolate bar category purchasing – and hence became highly effective as an advertising campaign for the Cadbury's brand. Capture the right dominant emotions and you will 'own' purchasing decisions in your category.

Interestingly, though, Cadbury's did not seem to fully understand why the Gorilla ad had become so successful (perhaps they were using conventional research?).

Rather than defining the dominant emotional goals as related to personal indulgence they focused on a feeling – joy – which is actually an outcome of achieving emotional goals. This is an important distinction because this subtle misunderstanding led to the creation of an advertising brief 'Rediscover the Joy' that could be interpreted via a number of different emotional routes, all of which can have a feeling of joy as an outcome.

To illustrate this crucial difference: think how different the joy of, say, motherhood is compared to different types of joy like the joy of discovery, or the joy of winning or the joy of snuggling up on the sofa with a good book and a cup of tea. All of these are 'joy' – but they are also very different emotionally. Which one is right for the brand? This ambiguity proved costly for Cadbury's.

Keen to reproduce the success of 'Gorilla', Cadbury briefed their agency to produce a follow-up ad written to the same brief of 'Rediscover the Joy' – and the advertisement that followed did indeed do this. You may recall it – it featured animated trucks at an airport racing each other along the runway to the soundtrack of Queen's 'Don't Stop Me Now'. The ad was like a mini action movie with the trucks all competing to win. The trucks were certainly having a great time racing each other – hence the 'Joy' brief was fulfilled – but not in the sense of moments of extreme personal pleasure or indulgence – rather their joy came from different goal drivers like Excitement, Adventure, Autonomy. Just take a look at the difference in emotional goal profile between the Cadbury's brand, the 'Trucks' ad and the 'Gorilla' ad:

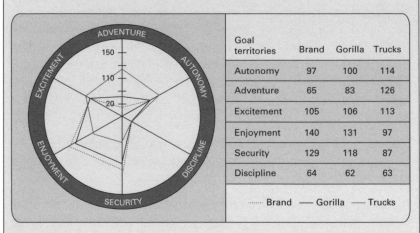

Goal territories	Brand	Gorilla	Trucks
Autonomy	97	100	114
Adventure	65	83	126
Excitement	105	106	113
Enjoyment	140	131	97
Security	129	118	87
Discipline	64	62	63

······ Brand —— Gorilla —— Trucks

Figure 4.2

As you can see clearly, the emotional goal profile of the 'Gorilla' ad is much closer to the emotional goal profile of the brand – whereas the 'Trucks' profile is very different. 'Trucks' activated emotions like adventure and autonomy which, while powerful, are just not relevant as emotional goal drivers in the chocolate category. 'Gorilla', by contrast, activates emotions that mirror those of the category – and hence was successful at driving preference for the Cadbury's brand. 'Trucks' was not able to do this, and this ad was quickly taken off air.

Not only does this case study illustrate the incredible power of associating your brand with the emotional goal drivers of category purchase (and doing so distinctively), it also illustrates how easy it is to get this wrong, and how conventional research tools often provide insights that are just not accurate.

It is very hard for companies who have become 'wedded' to conventional research to change – but if they are going to get these crucial positioning decisions right then they have to be open to using the new, neuropsychology-based tools that are becoming increasingly available.'

The Growth Director's Summary

Here's what you need to know about the brain science behind growth:

- In order to cope with complexity the vast majority of purchase decisions are taken subconsciously by our System 1 brains.
- Our brand choice decisions are driven by the perceived fit between the brands on offer and the dominant motivational goal which we are trying to satisfy.
- Motivational goals have two components: an explicit, functional component linked to the properties of brands in the category (e.g. cleaning or fragrance), and an implicit, emotional component linked to more general psychological goals (e.g. ensuring security or having fun).
- It is usually hard to differentiate meaningfully via explicit goals (since acceptable functional performance becomes the 'entry ticket' to the category which all brands must satisfy); successful differentiation is much more effectively achieved via 'owning' one of the category's dominant implicit, emotional goals.
- One simple way to think about the emotional goals that drive everything we do is in the following six categories: autonomy, adventure, discipline, security, enjoyment and excitement. All of our decision making is driven by some combination of these six goal territories.

- Our subconscious System 1 brains are very efficient at spotting the best fit between the goals we are trying to achieve and the brand choices available – this is how we make autopilot choices.
- Once chosen, autopilot preference tends to become reinforced by repeated usage and by increased sensitivity to that brand's advertising/marketing messages.
- Conventional research cannot connect with our sub-conscious brains and so is of limited use – and can often be misleading – in helping us understand the drivers of autopilot choice. Emerging research techniques leveraging latest neuroscientific learnings are increasingly able to do this.

Finding your Growth Sweet Spot: How most companies fail to focus on their biggest growth opportunities – and what to do about it

OK, let's look at what we have learned so far.

Hopefully, by this stage, it will be fairly clear that significant, sustained, profitable growth (Good Growth) is the single most valuable attribute that a business can have – but that most businesses are quite poor at delivering this.

We've examined some of the organisational reasons for this Growth Paradox and established that a lack of accountability for growth (in effect, the lack of a designated Growth Director) in most organisations often leads to a lack of executive focus on growth, a failure to develop and implement growth strategies and a failure to allocate the resources and management attention needed to deliver Good Growth.

We've also established that, beyond these organisational shortfalls most businesses make a common Big Growth Mistake which makes it very hard for them to grow consistently, and leads to significant wastage in their commercial and marketing plans. This Big Growth Mistake is the common assumption that all consumer purchases are potentially available and that the way to grow is to construct commercial and marketing plans that try to grab as many of these as possible. This false assumption typically leads to plans characterised by super busy promotional activity, unaffordably expensive retailer/distributor support, flip-flopping marketing/advertising campaigns and ineffective initiative plans that add cost and complexity to businesses – and usually fail to deliver profitable growth.

We have learned that this way of looking at how consumers shop is just plain wrong. In fact, most of the time, we shop on autopilot from a small portfolio of favourite brands that we have chosen subconsciously for largely emotional reasons and to which we stay super-loyal. Once we have chosen an autopilot, that brand will get 75%+ of our category purchases until something significant changes. This behaviour is hard-wired into our brains and it is very difficult to consciously change it. The key to growth is simply to learn how to position your brand to become the default autopilot choice of your target consumers – that's it.

We have further learned that understanding how to secure autopilot status is not easy. Autopilot choice is driven by our subconscious System 1 brains, autopilot decisions are made at a small number of Moments of Maximum Emotional Impact (MoMIs) and are driven as much by emotional factors as rational ones. As autopilot choice happens subconsciously, conventional research (which interacts mainly with our conscious System 2 brains) is not able to identify the moments when autopilot choices are made or to understand the complex mix of emotional/psychological/rational factors that lie behind them.

However, we have also seen that breakthroughs in understanding of how our subconscious brains work following the Nobel Prize-winning work of Daniel Kahneman in 2002 has enabled recent developments of neuroscience-based research tools that can begin to connect with our subconscious decision-making processes to enable us to identify and understand the moments when autopilot decisions are made.

So – there is hope!

What does it take to become an autopilot brand

There are just three fundamentals to positioning yourself to become the default autopilot choice of your target consumers:

1. You must *define the target consumers* for whom you want to become the default autopilot choice –not as straightforward as you might think.
2. You must understand how to make an *emotional connection* with these

consumers to give you 'permission to sell' at the key moments of autopilot choice.

3. You must offer them a *differentiated performance promise* that both connects meaningfully with the emotional drivers behind the moments when autopilot choices are made, and is believably different from/better than competitive brands.

The Growth Director says:
Here's what you have to do to become the default autopilot choice

- Define the target consumers with whom you want to become the default autopilot brand choice.
- Understand the MoMIs when autopilot decisions are made and the emotions that drive these.
- Understand how to make an emotional connection with these consumers at these key MoMIs to give you 'permission to sell' to them.
- Offer a differentiated performance promise that connects emotionally with your target consumers, is relevant to the identified MoMIs and is believably different from/better than those made by other brands.

We'll take each of these in turn: this chapter will cover the crucial area of targeting the right consumers, then Chapter 6 will go on to unpack the fundamentals of securing autopilot status by establishing a strong emotional connection with target consumers and offering them a performance advantage meaningful enough to secure their preference.

Remember first of all what the ultimate objective of this is – to find a way to optimise the growth trends of your business. So – the task of identifying your target customers comes down to asking yourself the question: 'With which consumers do we have the best chance of securing autopilot status?' since that will determine your likelihood of growing.

It should be immediately obvious that the answer to this question is not 'anyone who'll buy us'.

Recognise that, once you are clear about which group of consumers you are going to target, you will be tasked with developing and delivering a proposition that is so appealing to this group that it will secure your position as their default autopilot choice. And that's great, of course. But recognise also that, as you do this, you will inevitably be building a proposition that will not appeal to other groups of consumers – and in many cases there may be more consumers in the 'doesn't appeal' group than in the 'we love it' group. That's fine – as long as you are confident that your target group are (a) large enough to provide you with significant, profitable growth over a sustained period, and (b) likely to be open enough to what your brand can credibly promise that you have a decent chance of becoming their autopilot.

Later in this chapter we'll come back to the consequences of clearly prioritising one consumer group over another – and how this can be a very positive outcome as long as your choice of target consumers has been done correctly.

How do you go about defining the consumers with whom your growth prospects are brightest?

The key fundamental to remember in developing an effective targeting strategy is that *brand choice is driven by finding the brand which seems (to your subconscious brain) best able to satisfy the dominant emotional goals* in any given purchasing situation.

Remember that all our behaviour (not just our shopping behaviour) is driven by the desire to meet some combination of high-level emotional goals (see Chapter 4): security, enjoyment, excitement, adventure, autonomy and/or discipline.

In any given situation we will be seeking to meet some specific combination of these goals depending on our particular circumstances and preferences. So, illustrating this by taking the example of someone planning a holiday: a 20-something single person might be driven most by a goal combination dominated by excitement, adventure and, perhaps, autonomy; the goals of a family with young children would be more likely to emphasise things like enjoyment, excitement and, probably, security. In either case, their choice of holiday destination, accommodation, activities etc (in essence, their choice of holiday 'brand') would be guided by choosing the option that seemed to best enable them to meet their dominant goals. It is easy to see that the two holidays chosen are likely to be very different.

Most of the time, for the vast majority of purchase decisions we make on a daily basis, the choices between available options are nothing like as clear cut as the two holiday choices I suggested here. But the choice process is the same. Our subconscious System 1 brains will be very aware of what set of goals we are seeking to fulfil in any given situation, and will automatically guide us to choose the brand which has built an expectation that it can help us to fulfil these goals.

Which set of emotional goals (or which 'Emotional Goal Territory') are you aiming to become the default brand for?

This choice should be driven by answering three basic questions:

(a) *How big is the Emotional Goal Territory you are considering?* Crucially, is it big enough to deliver the growth you desire?
(b) *Does any other brand already 'own' this territory?* If so, you are unlikely to be able to become the autopilot there unless you are very confident you can achieve meaningful differentiation and clear preference.
(c) *How close a match is your brand's equity to the 'goal map' of the territory you are considering?* It would be very hard for Volvo to out-perform Mercedes as a brand to deliver 'excitement' and 'autonomy' – or for Mercedes to beat Volvo for 'safety/security'. Don't be tempted to target a territory that is a poor fit for your brand – even if this is the biggest territory in the market.

An easy way to conceptualise the goal combinations that drive all our behaviours – and all our purchasing decisions – is to think of them like a 'spider diagram' mapping the relative strength in any given situation of each of the six goal territories. To illustrate this lets go back to a product category I referred to earlier –deodorants/body sprays.

Many of the consumers choosing to make a purchase in this category would want to ensure that their deodorant was long lasting, effective in maintaining dryness and keeping them smelling fresh all day. Their 'goal map' would probably show dominance by goals linked to security, discipline, perhaps some autonomy.

For a small group however (probably mainly young single men aged 15–20) the dominant goals driving choice in this category are linked to making themselves more attractive to girls – so their 'goal map' would emphasise excitement, adventure and again maybe autonomy.

I've illustrated these two goal maps on the diagram below (borrowing the format, with permission, from Decode Marketing) with the 'confidence in all day dryness' map marked by a solid line and the 'seduction' map marked with a broken line.

The point is that the consumers whose goal map was closest to the solid spider diagram would be guided by their subconscious to choose

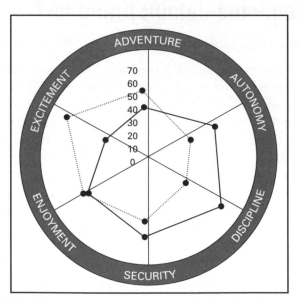

Figure 5.1 'Decode Goal Map'™ reproduced with permission of Decode Marketing.

(Solid Line: purchases driven by security/discipline/autonomy = 'dryness'

Broken Line: purchases driven by excitement/adventure/enjoyment = 'seduction')

a brand like Sure which would be confidently expected to keep them dry and fresh all day. The consumers whose goals were driven by a desire to enhance their seductiveness would almost certainly choose Lynx/ Axe. On the vast majority of occasions these choices would be made subconsciously as your System 1 brain matched brands to your particular goal map and guided you to the right choice for you.

In any category there will be a number of Emotional Goal Territories which describe the goal motivations of groups of consumers for buying into that category. Typically, in a consumer product category there might be five or six identifiable Emotional Goal Territories that represent the goal maps of significant groups of consumers (or, rather, of purchase occasions).

In a category such as deodorants/body sprays, perhaps the Emotional Goal Territories might look something like this:

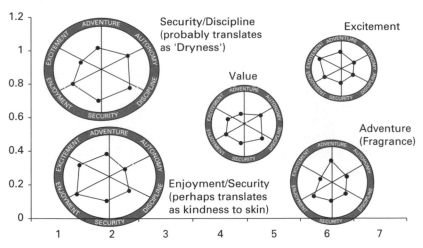

Figure 5.2

As you can see from this (speculative, but probably fairly close to the truth) illustration, you would typically see two or maybe three territories of significant size, accounting for the motivations of large numbers of consumers (or purchase occasions), plus two or three smaller 'niche' territories which account for a significant, but smaller, number of category purchases.

So, assuming the map above is broadly accurate, in the deodorant/body spray category the largest numbers of purchase occasions are accounted for by motivations driven by a desire for confidence in the 'dryness' delivered to the user, and by those driven by a desire for 'protection plus skin kindness'. Smaller quantities of purchase occasions are driven by consumers looking for a distinctive fragrance, by consumers seeking best value, and by the good old Lynx/Axe group looking to enhance their attractiveness.

Step 1 in understanding how to identify your highest-potential consumers is to complete a market map of this sort. Be clear on what Emotional Goal Territories exist in your category and how big (in terms of how many purchase occasions are driven by these goals) each is.

Towards the end of this chapter we will touch on some of the emerging techniques that allow you to complete this type of mapping with real confidence both in the validity of the territories identified and their relative size. Simply identifying which is the biggest Emotional Goal Territory in your category is only the first step. Clearly, if all brands tried to target the same consumers/goal motivations then most would lose out. In most mature consumer categories the largest territory tends to be 'owned' strongly by the incumbent market leading brand – by definition, that's how it became the market leader!

So, to go back to the deodorant example, the largest territory is likely to be driven by a desire for confident dryness, and this territory is already well populated with Sure 'owning' the bulk of the purchase occasions backed up by smaller brands like Arrid Extra Dry. Any other brand attempting to muscle in on this territory is likely to have a very hard fight since Sure has, over many years, established such strong dryness credentials, and these will have been reinforced many times over by our subconscious brains as we consume their advertising, experience the product etc.

Step 2 in developing a truly effective targeting strategy is to understand to what extent the goal motivations of each Emotional Goal Territory are owned by existing brands, and to what extent your own brand's equity could either currently, or with some tweaks, *meet these goals better than other brands and so become the autopilot choice* for all consumers/

purchase occasions driven by that territory's goals. This identifies the territory which is your brands 'Growth Sweet Spot'.

Returning again to the deodorant/body spray category and to Lynx/Axe, it is clear that, while it would not be credible for Lynx to try to out-do Sure on a superior dryness platform, the Lynx brand does have established equity as a brand for young men. Once it is understood that the biggest category goal motivation for that consumer group is linked to 'seduction', then the way is clear for Lynx to develop a proposition and commercial approach which seeks to own this territory (its Growth Sweet Spot). That, of course, is exactly what the brand has done.

Now – the Emotional Goal Territory best described as 'seduction' is a lot smaller than those representing 'dryness' or 'kindness to skin'. A brand that sets out to own this territory will, by definition, render itself unattractive to all those consumers/purchase occasions driven by other goals. In the case of Lynx, the territory was big enough to provide the growth they needed, and their equity fit was sufficiently good to enable them to credibly own this territory. These factors made this a brilliant piece of strategic targeting for this now very successful brand.

The crucial point that must be understood for truly effective targeting is that you MUST find the Emotional Goal Territory (or Territories) where your brand can credibly deliver against the dominant goals more effectively than competitors. This is what makes it your brand's Growth Sweet Spot – and to grow, you must focus relentlessly on this territory. Attempting to appeal to consumers who are motivated by goals for which your brand is a poor fit will almost inevitably end in a failure to grow – and to commercial plans relying on promotions and price-driven activity to maintain any sort of sales momentum.

This also helps to explain why incumbent market leaders are so difficult for smaller brands to compete with. In any mature market, the brand which best delivers against the dominant motivational goals in the biggest emotional goal territory will, by definition, have become the market leader. Over time, the connections in our subconscious brains between this brand and delivery of the key goals will be reinforced by its advertising, by usage of the product, by its predominance in-store etc. As we explained in Chapter 4, the subconscious brain is stubborn, and reluctant to change its mind once it has been made up, so these connections become stronger and stronger over time.

This means that, even if a new brand appears which is technically able to meet the territory goals even more effectively than the incumbent, it is very difficult indeed to persuade our System 1 brains that the 'new kid on the block' is preferable.

A memorable example of this occurred for me back in the early 1990s when I was working at Procter and Gamble.

One of the few cleaning categories in which we did not have a major brand was domestic bleach – the category was dominated by Domestos, which was Unilever's long-time market leader. Domestos had been positioned for many years on a strong platform of guaranteed germ kill – its slogan was 'Kills 99% of Household Germs – Dead' and this had been reinforced repeatedly by its hard-hitting advertising, its uncompromising packaging design, and its thick product and strong fragrance.

The category was all about providing mums with high confidence that their families would be kept safe from germs – the emotional goal map would have been dominated by the discipline and security motivations.

Our clever scientists in the P&G labs, however, came up with a breakthrough. They managed to develop a radically different bleach formulation which was able to cling to the sides of the toilet bowl for much longer – even after repeated flushes. This, of course, meant that they could produce a bleach that could 'out-Domestos Domestos' by promising even better germ kill for longer. Wow!! Let's go!!

And so we did. We launched our 'Vortex' bleach with huge marketing support in a full frontal assault on the market-leading Domestos brand.

Our advertising showed powerful side-by-side comparisons of toilet bowls cleaned with Vortex and with Domestos – and showing how the Domestos-cleaned toilet left more germs than that cleaned using Vortex. It all seemed hugely logical – and it was. But, of course, our strategy took no account of the emotional side of brand choice.

While we could technically out-do Domestos on the core category benefit of germ-kill, our full frontal assault on its Emotional Goal Territory was doomed to failure. All the clever scientific 'proof' in the world could not undo all those years of emotionally powerful connections that had been forged between Domestos and the dominant emotional goals of discipline and security. And, of course, since the neuroscience to enable us to understand this was not yet available, we were unable to see our mistake.

So we ploughed on for year after year, unable to understand why, with a technically superior product and huge slugs of marketing investment we were unable to shift consumer loyalty to Domestos. We never made any significant impact on Domestos' market share – and never managed to establish Vortex as a meaningful competitor. A classic targeting mistake.

Had today's understanding of how our brains work been available to us we would (at least I hope we would!) have realised that attempting to 'muscle in' in such direct fashion on a goal territory with such a well-established incumbent was most unlikely to succeed. Rather, if the bleach category was a strategic priority for the business, we should have tried to identify other goal territories where there was no super-strong incumbent – and developed a proposition (almost certainly not competing with Domestos on superior germ-kill) that would deliver against the goal combination that was dominant in these territories.

Who knows – we might have come up with a truly differentiated proposition that appealed to a very different set of emotional goals – as innovative products like Toilet Duck (made by SC Johnson) did a few years later.

So – a salutary lesson about how painful, and expensive, a lack of effective targeting can be.

To get it right, you need to be able to answer accurately those three key questions that were posed earlier in the chapter:

• How big is the Emotional Goal Territory you are considering?
• Does any other brand already 'own' this territory?
• How close a match is your brand's equity to the 'goal map' of the territory you are considering?

Get these questions right and you will be well on the way to identifying the highest potential consumer group for your brand – your Growth Sweet Spot.

A crucial targeting point

Despite what the Lynx/Axe example might seem to imply, the key to targeting is NOT to select a particular socio-demographic and focus on that. This is the classic targeting mistake that most businesses continue to make, even those who do think seriously about the subject.

Remember what we learned in Chapter 4 about how our brains work. Our purchase decisions are NOT driven by who we are, where we live, what we earn etc. Rather, they are driven by the emotional goals that we are trying to satisfy at any given time – and, for every one of us, *these goals can change depending on the context of the purchase decisions we are taking.*

I illustrate this via an example from another typical consumer product category – ice cream. Is our choice of ice-cream product driven by our socio-demographics – where we live/what we earn/our sex/our age? Rarely. Rather, it will be driven by the goal context at the point of purchase.

If we are buying ice-cream for ourselves and our children while out together perhaps we will choose products/brands that are fun and enjoyable but also good value – like cornets or ice lollies (from the Goal Territory analysis, maybe that's a mixture of the goals of enjoyment and discipline).

If we are out on our own and want to have an indulgent ten minutes on a park bench, perhaps we will choose an up-market/exotic Magnum (perhaps that involves goals like adventure and autonomy).

If we are buying for a family dinner at home we might buy a tub of easy-to-share soft scoop ice-cream (maybe the goals here are around security/enjoyment).

If we're buying for a dinner party with friends we want to impress, then maybe we'll go for an expensive Italian product as an accompaniment to our immaculately crafted home-made pudding (perhaps that's driven by adventure or excitement).

The point is that if we tried to define our target group by socio-demographics, we would be likely to choose a group who, at different times, would make each of these purchase choices. How would that help us to develop a differentiated proposition that they would prefer and choose on autopilot?

The key is to choose as your Growth Sweet Spot a goal territory which is dominant for a large proportion of the purchase decisions in the category. Often (as with Lynx/Axe), that will apply predominantly to a particular socio-demographic – and that makes life easier. But it is the goal territory you must focus on, NOT the socio-demographic profile.

The Growth Director says:

Target consumers by Emotional Goal Territories, NOT by socio-demographics

- Brand choice is driven by the search for a brand that best enables you to satisfy the dominant emotional goals in any given purchasing situation.
- To maximise your potential for growth you must find an Emotional Goal Territory (a) which is big enough to deliver the growth you desire and (b) where your brand's equity is at least as good a fit as the equity of competing brands.
- AVOID territories (even large ones) where an established competitor has a very close fit to the emotional drivers of purchase. You will not win there!
- The emotional goals driving purchase decisions change according to our circumstances. Target Emotional Goal Territories – NOT socio-demographic consumer groups.

To go back to the Lynx/Axe example, the Growth Sweet Spot goal territory could probably be best described as 'seduction'. Now it just so happens that this goal territory is dominant for a particular socio-demographic – young men. But, by targeting this territory you will attract all those whose purchasing (or, more importantly, their autopilot choice) is driven by that dominant goal.

In the ice-cream example the goal territory would not 'map' onto one particular socio-demographic – but would attract consumers from a whole variety of backgrounds in circumstances where this combination of goal territories became dominant.

Targeting by goal territory, NOT socio-demographics is key.

The final important point to make about targeting is that truly effective, goal-based targeting can deliver fantastic growth for a brand even when the very act of sharpening the targeting focus excludes large groups of consumers. With apologies for returning to the same example, the Lynx/Axe case study is a brilliant example of this.

It's clear that the genius of Lynx/Axe's targeting was in identifying as its Growth Sweet Spot a group of consumers – young men – who had a specific goal that drove their purchasing behaviour in the category – that of attracting young women. By deciding to focus against this group Lynx/Axe implicitly recognised that it would lead them to develop a proposition that, while it might have high appeal to young men, would have little/no appeal to many other consumer groups in the deodorant/body spray market – and indeed would be likely to be a turn-off for many of them. That's exactly what their highly sexualised, very male-orientated proposition did.

In the case of Lynx, this 'alienation' of non-target consumer groups just did not matter commercially, because the proposition was so motivating to their target group, and the target group were plenty big enough to deliver all the growth the brand needed. Great targeting – so much more powerful than trying to craft a bland 'makes everyone a little more attractive' proposition that might have had a better chance with older men, parents, women, grandparents etc.

So – this chapter should by now have established the importance and commercial power of developing a clear targeting strategy that focuses your commercial activity on that group of consumers/purchase occasions where your brand best fits the emotional goals they are looking to satisfy – your Growth Sweet Spot. The obvious challenge this raises, though, is how can this be done accurately since the goal territories are driven mainly by emotional, not rational, factors, and the 'matching' between brand equity and the goal motivations behind each territory is done in the vast majority of cases by our subconscious System 1 brains.

The first thing to say is that this work can be attempted using conventional research techniques like consumer surveys, focus groups, accompanied shopping trips, one-to-one depth interviews etc. While consumers find it very hard to articulate their emotional drivers in any situation, and while it is impossible for them to understand how their subconscious brains are working, most categories are simple enough that a broad understanding of goal territories, their size and the key emotional drivers behind them can be derived from conventional work and from good old-fashioned getting close to all available consumer data.

The extremely successful targeting work completed at Boots in the mid-2000s and described elsewhere in this chapter was all done utilising conventional research – focus groups and one-to-one interviews plus significant work with consumer surveys to 'size' the different market sectors/consumer groups. There are many other similarly successful examples using conventional research techniques.

But – conducting targeting in this way is risky, and far too likely to lead to error. We are rational beings and find it very hard to ascribe any of our actions to emotional causes. We also massively over-estimate the extent to which our purchasing decisions and brand choices are made rationally utilising our conscious System 2 brains. The potential for misleading conclusions from targeting exercises using conventional tools is significant.

To take the Vortex/Domestos bleach example described above – all of the conventional research work we had done with consumers had told us that a brand promising 'even better germ kill than Domestos' was a sure-fire winner. When consumers responded to our research questions with their rational System 2 brains they naturally told us that they would of course buy a new brand that could deliver this superior performance.

What rational person would say anything else?

The reality, of course, was that despite their rational System 2 brains telling them that it made good sense to buy the new brand Vortex, their stubborn, subconscious System 1 brain was digging its heels in, effectively saying 'but we like Domestos ... we trust Domestos ... Domestos has never let us down ... we don't want to take the risk of trying this new brand' (or words to that effect . . .) and, as almost always happens, System 1 prevailed. Of course, since our conventional research tools could not connect with System 1 we missed this crucial truth – costing the company many years of hard and frustrating work and many millions of wasted pounds in unproductive product development work and inefficient marketing spending.

Fortunately for today's business decision-makers, neuroscience is beginning to provide new ways for us to conduct this work with much higher degrees of insight and certainty. It is not the purpose of this book to describe these in any detail. However, tools now do exist which enable us to identify the Emotional Goal Territories in every market, to size them (in terms of the % of category purchases that they drive), to understand the emotions that lie behind them and to identify the consumer/occasion/circumstances combinations that are driven by the emotional goal combinations in each territory.

Whether you choose to be brave and employ some of the emerging neuro-science based tools, or whether you take a punt on the old conventional research methods, effective consumer targeting is absolutely crucial to any business seriously interested in orientating itself for growth. No business can effectively appeal to all consumers in all situations. Businesses that try to do this end up with bland, undifferentiated propositions and end up getting picked off by more targeted competitors. If you are not clear about who you want to be the autopilot choice for, then your chances of producing a truly compelling proposition that will drive significant, sustained, profitable growth is very small indeed.

So let's assume that you have done this and identified your target consumer group and the Emotional Goal Territories that drive the bulk of their purchasing occasions. You now need to turn to developing an understanding of how to build a proposition that will secure autopilot status with this group. And that's the subject of Chapter 6.

Case Study: Betty, Tina and Charlotte Come to Boots; *Andy Brent, ex CMO Boots*

'Back in the mid-2000s I worked as CMO for Boots the Chemist. During my time in this role, I was involved in a piece of targeting work that was truly transformational for the business, and which illustrates very well the power in getting this crucial area of business strategy right.

Boots, as everyone knows, sells health, beauty and personal care products (and sandwiches . . .). And Boots is a store at which just about everyone shops. How do you implement meaningful targeting with a store that serves everyone?

When I joined Boots, the business was struggling and was losing share to the supermarkets who were attacking aggressively via heavy discounting of popular products. Year after year they took share from us in each of our core categories – health, beauty and personal care. Sales declined, customer numbers and frequency of shopping fell, market share went south, profits suffered.

Boots had many problems at the time – crowded, hard-to-shop stores; product ranges with little genuinely exciting differentiation; commercial programmes driven by a combination of striving to secure supplier funding to enhance margins with a heavy reliance on expensive promotions to drive sales; uncompetitive pricing vs the supermarkets. All serious issues in themselves.

But at the heart of these problems lay a classic targeting issue – Boots had forgotten who it was for.

Part of the problem is that 'everyone' shops at Boots at some point – men, women, young, old, singles, families and all combinations thereof. With sales under constant pressure the company had got locked into a desperate cycle of trying to 'please all the people all the time' – and was, consequently, really pleasing nobody.

The business wanted to drive its profitable and distinctive beauty product ranges – but did not want to create an environment where men would feel uncomfortable.

It wanted to attract healthcare business from older shoppers – but did not want to 'give up' store space to healthcare products when it could be used to feature promotions on high-selling toiletries.

It wanted to feature interesting new product initiatives – but not at the expense of giving promotional 'end displays' to the promotions suppliers were prepared to pay a good price to 'rent' each week.

So, as often happens when target customer focus is unclear, Boots ended up losing sales and share each month to its supermarket and other competitors.

When I joined Boots the problem was clear – but the business did not know how to resolve the dilemma of 'how do we improve our targeting without losing sales with the non-targeted groups?' Richard Baker, the CEO at the time, asked me to lead work to recommend how the business should sharpen its customer targeting in order to re-establish preference with core consumer groups and turn the declining sales trends around.

Together with my marketing and research teams we set about talking to consumers, interrogating the (masses) of good consumer data that the company had accumulated, collating and examining external data on market trends, and talking extensively to key stakeholders within the business (tip: in almost all cases incumbent management know much more than they think they do about their business' problems, and the alternative solutions). The process was intensive and took about three months. At the end of it we had a clear view of who our target customers were. We identified three simple groups and, to make the outputs easily memorable, we gave them a 'BTC' ('Boots the Chemist') acronym: we called them Betty, Tina and Charlotte.

Betty was our older woman primarily concerned with healthcare for herself and (often) her husband. She was potentially very profitable since she needed increasing amounts of prescription medicines and associated treatments. She wanted a Boots that provided friendly, expert healthcare advice in her neighbourhood in a calm shopping environment she would feel comfortable in.

Tina was our mum with kids. She visited very frequently and shopped the whole store. She loved the Advantage Card and promotional offers. She valued convenience and speed of shopping – and lots of deals. She accounted for the biggest share of purchases in the store – and the stores were set up more for her needs than any other shopper. But – she was (and this was a big surprise to the business) unprofitable, skewing heavily towards promotions and low-margin big brands, rarely being able to afford the more expensive beauty products and having relatively limited need for profitable prescription medicines.

Charlotte we defined as 'the 29-year-old woman inside every woman' who, from time to time and whatever her age/circumstances wanted to feel, and be told she was looking gorgeous. She was most interested in beauty products and advice and wanted to shop in a premium, high-service environment. And, Charlotte was a profitable customer for Boots. Importantly (and without really realising the power of this at the time) we were identifying 'Charlotte' as an emotional need state that almost all women were in from time to time – not as a simple socio-demographic definition.

This simple, very high-level piece of targeting immediately brought a clarity to the business that proved transformational.

It immediately became clear that we had been setting our stores up, and developing our commercial plans for a customer group (Tina) who, while very frequent shoppers, were predominantly unprofitable. Meeting Tina's needs was reducing our appeal to the two less visible but more profitable groups Betty and Charlotte. The re-focusing of the business against these two very different but very important groups required some radical change – but delivered a turnaround in the business' fortunes, restoring strong growth and driving profits.

Some of the key changes made in the beauty elements of Boots offers are described elsewhere in this book – but to illustrate how targeting clarity can lead to radical but highly effective change, here's how we re-positioned our healthcare business to serve the needs of our 'Bettys'.

Betty wanted a slower, more thoughtful shopping experience that enabled her to browse products that might be helpful to her without heavy promotional pressure. She wanted to be able to talk to friendly, expert healthcare professionals who would have time to listen to her worries and suggest treatments for them – and with whom she could build a relationship over time. And she wanted to be able to pick up information and advice that she could take home, consider and then come back in to talk about – even if no product purchase was involved.

For Betty, the Boots habit of siting the most popular healthcare products in the most prominent part of the store (to showcase promotional offers to 'fight' with the supermarkets) was not at all attractive – in fact it was a turn-off. She did not want to be forced into busy aisles full of younger shoppers rushing in and out of store, perhaps pushing past her with buggies or shopping trollies, and where it was difficult to find the products she really wanted.

Betty wanted quieter areas of the store focused on healthcare only. She wanted areas where she could sit down and talk to healthcare advisers – and she wanted staff with the time and the interest to do this. She wanted product layouts that made finding favourites easy and which did not 'confuse her' with lots of promotional displays and special offers. And she wanted information and advice much more than she wanted 'Buy One Get Second Half Price'.

Crucially, we knew that as well as being a potentially profitable group, Boots had a strong emotional connection with Betty – she instinctively liked and trusted us more than the supermarkets when it came to health matters, and so (although we didn't describe it in these terms) we knew that, if we got it right, we could become a very strong 'autopilot' for her – and this would deliver real growth.

So, based upon this targeting decision we changed our approach to healthcare, healthcare marketing and indeed to the healthcare areas of our stores.

Wherever feasible, we moved healthcare to the back of store, away from the busy, promotionally heavy, front-of-store areas. In the larger stores we created small private consultation areas where shoppers could sit with healthcare staff to discuss their worries and needs. We changed the staffing and training of our pharmacists and healthcare teams so that they saw their role more as interacting with customers than simply 'counting and dispensing pills'. We created suites of free information on common healthcare issues that our shoppers could take away, consider and use to initiate later discussions – marketed as 'The Boots Health Club'.

This simple act of targeting clarity turned the Boots healthcare business around. Suddenly, rather than competing with the supermarkets on the basis of who could offer deeper discounts on popular vitamin ranges and cough mixtures we began to offer our target shoppers a differentiated proposition that played to Boots' equity and which could never be credibly matched in a busy supermarket environment. This fitted very accurately with the emotional goals that drove them when they were shopping for healthcare products.

Sales stabilised, then grew. Visit frequency of this older shopper group grew significantly. Size of average healthcare purchase grew . . . and kept growing. And, as our differentiated proposition established itself we found we were attracting much more interest and support from producers of the key consumer brands – and, as any retailer will tell you, that's never a bad thing from a margin point of view!

This highly targeted approach led ultimately to the development of a new healthcare-focused format for small stores that we rolled out across the UK. This format – we called them 'Your Local Boots Pharmacy' – is now in over 1,000 stores across the country – and remains highly successful to this day.

The key to this case study is the targeting element. Without the clarity of deciding to focus on a particular consumer group, and accepting that this might put some other consumers off, we would never have arrived at a truly differentiated proposition that enabled us to turn around a declining business.

Accurate consumer targeting is absolutely key to delivering growth in any business situation – businesses forget this truth at their peril.'

The Growth Director's Summary

- To become the autopilot choice of your target consumers you must:
  - identify and understand the Moments of Maximum Emotional Impact when autopilot choices are made;
  - understand how to connect emotionally at these MoMIs; and
  - offer a differentiated performance promise that is believably different from/better than your competitors.

- To choose the part of your market that you should target to become the default autopilot choice you must understand:

  - How big is the Emotional Goal Territory you are considering? Crucially, is it big enough to deliver the growth you desire?
  - Does any other brand already 'own' this territory? If so, you are unlikely to be able to become the autopilot there unless you are very confident you can achieve meaningful differentiation and clear preference.
  - How close a match is your brand's equity to the 'goal map' of the territory you are considering?

- To find the Emotional Goal Territory with the greatest growth potential for your brand – your Growth Sweet Spot – you must find a territory where your brand's equity is at least as good a fit as other competing brands. Do NOT compete in territories where an incumbent fits the emotional goal profile better than you do.
- Remember: target Emotional Goal Territories NOT consumer groups. Emotional goals change according to circumstances and so targeting consumers will lead to ineffective commercial plans and inefficient marketing programmes.
- In mapping markets for Emotional Goal Territories consider using neuroscience-based research. Conventional research cannot connect easily with our emotions and is likely to provide misleading insights.

Chapter 6

Becoming an Autopilot Brand. How to secure automatic, and lasting, purchase preference for your brand

Chapter 5 explained the crucial importance of identifying very precisely who your target consumers are – which group of consumers/which set of consumer goal motivations represent the best chance for your brand to become the default autopilot and thus generate significant, sustained profitable growth.

Chapter 5 also explored how you might go about doing this – by mapping the Emotional Goal Territories that drive purchase decisions in your market and identifying the one or two where your brand's equity has the best fit – and indeed has a potentially better fit than all its competitors. That's your 'Growth Sweet Spot'.

Finally, Chapter 5 outlined the limitations of conventional research (which interacts primarily with our conscious, System 2 brains) in facilitating this mapping work, and described how new techniques using neuroscience-based tools can, for the first time, connect with our subconscious System 1 brains which are responsible for almost all our autopilot decisions.

With or without neuroscience-based tools, however (and I strongly recommend that you do use these tools if you can) most businesses will be able to complete a market mapping exercise and will thus be able to identify their Growth Sweet Spot and the Sweet Spot Customers who represent their best chance of securing default autopilot status and driving significant growth.

This now brings us to the most important challenge addressed in this book – once your target customers are efficiently identified, how do you go about developing and bringing to market a proposition that will enable you to secure autopilot status?

Remember that once you have identified those target customers there are two essential components to becoming their autopilot choice:

1. You must understand how to make an *emotional connection* with these consumers to give you 'permission to sell'.
2. You must make them a *differentiated performance promise* that both connects meaningfully with the emotional drivers behind the key moments when autopilot choices are made, and is believably different from/better than competitive brands.

Establishing an emotional connection with these consumers to give you 'permission to sell'

'Permission to sell?' What does that mean? Surely the whole way that commercial markets work is that we sell whenever and wherever we can – we certainly don't need to ask permission to do so. Well, maybe there is no legal requirement to ask for this permission but, unfortunately for many consumer-facing companies, unless it is obtained, our best efforts to persuade consumers to buy our products just will not get listened to. This goes back, again, to how our brains work.

Remember, around 90–95% of all the decisions we make are driven by our subconscious System 1 brains–and System 1 is driven as much (perhaps more) by emotional motivations as by rational arguments.

Remember also – crucially – how stubborn our System 1 brains are when they have made a judgment about something. The Muller Lyer Illusion that I used in Chapter 4 (the two lines that appeared to be of different lengths but are actually the same) shows very powerfully how, once our System 1 brain has made a judgment, it is very reluctant to change its mind – and is actively resistant to doing so even when it is presented with evidence to the contrary.

Crucially, this stubbornness is exacerbated when the attempt to change our minds about something is done in a purely rational way. Our System 1 brain reaches its conclusions by finding the best possible fit between a set of alternatives and the emotional goals that we are trying to meet in any given situation. While rationality (facts, demonstrations of performance, the actual lengths of two lines) plays a role in this decision, emotional factors are typically more important, and are the dominant drivers of most of the decisions (and certainly the vast majority of brand choice decisions) we ever make.

Any attempt to persuade or change the mind of our purely rational System 1 brains is likely to be rejected. Not because it is wrong, but because it does not feel relevant to the way System 1 made the decision in the first place. As it does not feel relevant, and because System 1 does not 'want' to be forced to change a decision with which is it perfectly happy, our subconscious will not only reject such an approach but will construct 'counter-arguments' to buttress its existing position. This phenomenon is commonly observed and much commented on amongst people who have studied neuroscience and how the brain works:

> Consumers may have built-in resistance to persuasive messages ... that can produce reverse priming effects. Are your marketing messages speaking to your consumers' conscious minds but creating resistance in their nonconscious minds?
>
> Genco et al (2013)

It is further likely that this pre-programmed propensity to reject rational attempts to persuade has been strongly reinforced in the last 30 or 40 years by a societal view that to admit to having been persuaded by an ad is 'wrong' or shows you to be an unsophisticated, naïve person. Most people will tell others that they 'don't fall for advertising claims' or 'aren't influenced by ads', and while this is almost certainly never true, it will have reinforced the resistance of our subconscious brains to rational selling attempts.

And yet ... we all know that all of us are influenced, from time to time, by great ads or are drawn to brands that we somehow just feel 'are right' for us. How does this happen?

Well, while System 1 is clearly resistant to changing its mind, it obviously does do this from time to time – and of course this makes sense. After all, without the capacity to change we would be condemned to making the same mistakes time after time (ok–I know sometimes it still feels like this . . .).

The key to influencing System 1 is to connect with it on the terms in which it deals. So – using the Muller Lyer Illusion again – a much more persuasive way to get the subconscious brain to 'see' the two lines as the same length would simply be to turn the fins on the lower line so that they point outward rather than inward. Immediately, System 1 would recognise and accept the cues it was using to decide which line is longer, and would decide that they are actually the same length.

Where brand choice is concerned, the decision-making cues are almost always emotional ones linking to the dominant goals of the relevant territory. Remember, in choosing between brands, System 1 is selecting the brand that it believes will best enable it to meet the dominant emotional goals that drive us to make a category purchase in the first place. If you cannot connect with System 1 on this emotional basis then your rational arguments for preference, however well-founded, will be rejected.

If, however, you can connect with and appropriate for your brand the emotions that lie behind the goals driving purchase decisions in your category – well then you have automatic 'permission to sell' and an opportunity to achieve significant growth with all consumers whose purchase decisions are driven by these goals.

To do this, you need to find 'Insights' that reveal core truths about how consumers feel about the products in your category and when and why those products are most emotionally important to them. 'Insights' are talked about often in business and in the marketing world in particular. For the purposes of the analysis in this book, I define 'insights' as *core consumer truths that reveal when/explain why your product's or service's performance is of such emotional importance to consumers.*

If you can present your product or service in the context of a powerful insight then this will enable you to 'unlock' consumers emotionally and give you the vital permission to sell that is often denied. If the insight is powerful enough, then simply identifying your brand with it may secure autopilot status.

> ### The Growth Director says:
> *Present your product in the context of 'Insights' to secure consumers' 'permission to sell'*
>
> - We are all hard-wired to resist attempts to sell to us. We have made brand choices we are comfortable with and are emotionally reluctant to risk changing.
> - Consumers are significantly more likely to listen to brand sales pitches if they feel an emotional connection with the brand – in other words if they feel the brand 'understands them'.
> - Key to establishing this connection is presenting your brand in the context of Insights that show you understand and empathise with your target consumer.
> - 'Insights' are core consumer truths that reveal when/explain why your product's performance is of most emotional importance to its users.
> - Presenting your brand in the context of powerful Insights will unlock consumers emotionally and give you 'permission to sell' to them.

Let's look at a couple of brands that have done this spectacularly well.

We will start with a brand which was already well established and successful, but found a way to step-change its rate of growth by forging a much deeper connection with the emotional goals of its target consumers and, for a period at least, becoming a truly dominant autopilot in its category – Dove cosmetics and its 'Campaign for Real Beauty'.

Dove's 'Campaign for Real Beauty'

Prior to this campaign, Dove was already a successful brand – but did not particularly stand out from its competitors in appealing to its target consumers – young to middle-aged women. The 'Campaign for Real Beauty' changed all that.

The genius of the campaign lay in a deep understanding of the emotional goals women were trying to fulfill when they chose beauty products, and finding a way to forge a unique connection with these goals.

Contrary to the impression you might get from viewing most of the advertising output of the beauty industry, the vast majority of women are not driven by a desire to look as good as a supermodel – particularly when it comes to everyday beauty products like skin treatments, toiletries etc. Rather, the emotional goal driving most women on a daily basis is to feel confident just as they are. Typically, they use beauty products not expecting a transformation in their appearance, but rather wanting to find a beauty regime that simply enables them to feel happy and comfortable in their own skin.

In fact, many of the women in Dove's target group, (women with 'normal' figures, features and complexions) were quietly frustrated at being bombarded with images of super-slim, super-good-looking women in films, magazines and, especially, advertisements by the beauty industry. While on the one hand these images did generate some aspirational desire to look better, they also led to a frustrated sense that, for the vast majority of 'normal' women, whatever they did they were never going to reach the 'beauty ideal' that was being presented to them. More importantly, this is not what they were trying to achieve when they went about their everyday lives.

Dove's campaign was different, and connected powerfully with the real emotional drivers of everyday beauty products for women. Not only did it celebrate 'normal' beauty by using a range of models with height/weight/complexions/features that weren't 'magazine-perfect', it also consistently showed them in groups, having fun together and completely at ease with their appearance.

There was no sense in any of the ads of 'I wish I was a bit slimmer/a bit more curvy/ a bit blonder/a bit taller etc'. Rather there was a joyous sense of 'I love who I am . . . and I'm having fun with my friends just as I am'.

Emotionally, this incredibly powerful insight struck a huge chord with most women. At last they had a brand that understood how they wanted to feel about themselves, which validated the way they looked right now – not one that was trying to make them discontented with the way nature had made them. *That's the sort of brand they wanted to do business with.*

Importantly, by consistently showing its models in group situations where they were clearly relaxed/at ease/having fun together, Dove connected powerfully with the true emotional drivers in the category for these women: not a desire to look as drop-dead gorgeous as a supermodel, but rather to be able to be relaxed about their own appearance and have fun with the people they value the most.

In other words, by showing that it approached the issue of feminine beauty in a way that was sympathetic to and empathetic with the emotional goal drivers of its target consumers, Dove obtained their 'permission to sell' and established an emotional bond between Dove and its consumers that differentiated it hugely from its more traditionally minded competitors.

While the marketing support for this campaign was strong, its PR impact dwarfed the impact of the brand's bought media. Women everywhere noticed, connected with the campaign and wanted their friends to notice it too. Dove had achieved the highest-level goal of every marketing campaign – to turn consumers into advocates.

Sales and market share responded. US brand sales in the two years following the 2004 launch of the Campaign for Real Beauty grew +12.5% and +10.1% respectively – spectacular results in a mature and highly competitive consumer market. The impact on featured products was more spectacular still – sales of the firming cream featured in one of the early billboard ads increased over 700% from 280,000 bottles to 2.3million bottles in the six months following the campaign's launch.

Remember – these results were achieved 'merely' with a new campaign that forged a powerful emotional bond between Dove and its consumers. No huge new breakthrough products. No big price cuts. No new promotional ideas. Simply a truly powerful connection with the emotional goal drivers behind their purchasing behaviour that made Dove's target consumers feel as if they'd found a brand they really wanted to do business with – a brand that became, very swiftly, their dominant autopilot choice.

The story of Felix

'Felix' is a brand of cat food produced by Nestlé Purina (previously Spillers) in the UK. Some years ago it was a distant number 2 in the market behind Mars' dominant market leader Whiskas. By working out how to connect to the dominant emotional goals driving the category, however, Felix found a way to transform its position, building 10 share points in two years and becoming the market leader.

I'll let Rob Murray, at the time the commercial director of Spillers in the UK and MD in Ireland (and recently CEO of the Lion Nathan brewing business in Australia), tell the story:

Case Study: How Emotional Insights Drive Growth – The story of felix; *by Rob Murray, Ex Commercial Director Spillers*

'When I came into the business the pet food category – largely driven by the approach Mars was taking – treated dog owners and cat owners the same. The team at Spillers had begun to challenge this paradigm but we had much work still to do.

Looking after dogs is a largely functional task. They need regular food as fuel and they'll eat most of what you give them. They need regular exercise, and they're always ready to be taken for a long walk. And they need lots of affection – and will always return it. Simply by entering the room a dog owner can be certain he/she will be showered with dog devotion!

Cats, however, are very different. Cats tend to be much fussier eaters and will happily walk away if they don't like what they're offered. They are fiercely independent and live life on their own terms – it's not uncommon for cats to unilaterally leave home and go and live elsewhere if they feel they've found a 'better offer' – dogs would never do that. One aspect vital to our Felix success was to make cat food that was incredibly palatable to cats.

Most importantly, though, cats are very sparing with their affections – and consequently cat owners crave those occasional moments when it appears their cat is demonstrating its love for them. For dog owners this affection is a given – for cat owners it's an occasional, precious reward.

So – while winning affection from your pet is not a dominant emotional goal for dog owners, it absolutely is for cat owners – and this crucial insight was essential for us in overhauling Whiskas and taking Felix to market leadership.

This insight enabled us to understand that what cat owners wanted more than anything else was a way to secure those moments of affection from their cats. Once we understood this we spent a lot of time identifying what those moments were. We found there were a small number of emotionally super powerful moments when overt displays of affection meant a huge amount.

For example – that moment when a cat seeks you out, rubs around your legs and asks to be stroked. In all likelihood the cat is asking to be fed – but to the owner it feels like, after having been ignored for most the day, their cat is finally demonstrating its love for them.

Similarly, we found that a lot of cats run to greet their owner when they return home from a trip out. Again, it may well be that the cat is actually saying 'about time . . . when are you going to feed me?' – but to the owner this again feels like one of those rare moments of genuine affection.

By understanding this we were able to build our marketing approach around bringing these moments to life, using our animated 'Felix' character to do this. Suddenly, we found we were connecting in a new, much more powerful way with our target consumers. We were connecting with the emotional goals that drove them in their choice of cat food – winning affection from their cats – in a way that our more functionally-driven competitors like Whiskas were not.

Once we had secured this 'permission to sell' we were able to explain how our cat food products were preferred by cats/healthier for cats – and we were listened to in a way that more rational 'selling approaches' from other brands were not. In effect, we made our food the 'gateway' to the emotional connection that cat owners wanted with their pets – and that made our cat food products the ones that consumers suddenly decided they wanted.

Our emotionally-driven approach was in stark contrast to traditional competitors like Whiskas that continued to explain rationally how their products had been developed by scientists to be better for cats or how cat experts recommended their products.

All great – and perfectly fine rational propositions. But completely lacking in an emotional connection with the reason cat owners chose one brand over another – and so despite all the investment that companies like Mars made in their advertising campaigns, often not really listened to.

And the results? Well they were spectacular. In two years we built Felix share by around 10 share points, and took market leadership from Whiskas for the first time ever.

An incredibly powerful example of how important it is to establish that emotional connection with consumers. Without it, you are unlikely to even make it into their consideration set.'

For a final example of the difference that uncovering insights that enable you to forge an emotional connection with the emotional goal drivers behind a category can make take a look at the Coca Cola case study in the box below – even the biggest, most established brands in the world need to remember that without this emotional connection they will find becoming autopilot and growing much more difficult.

Case Study: Restoring growth at Coca-Cola through propositional change; *by Phil Anderton, Global Brand Manager Coca Cola 1996–1998*

Phil has worked in senior marketing positions in major companies all over the world, including five years at Procter and Gamble and some seven years working for Coca-Cola in the US and in Europe including a spell as Global Brand Manager for Coca-Cola (Coke) in the 1990s.

Phil has also been Chief Marketing Officer of the ATP World Tour, CEO of Scottish Rugby and of Hearts Football Club, and CEO of Al Jazira in the Emirates.

In Chapter 2, Phil described how The Big Growth Mistake caused years of static sales trends at Coke, culminating in the notoriously unsuccessful launch of New Coke in the late 1980s. Here, Phil explains how a fundamental brand repositioning driven by powerful consumer insights turned the Coke business around.

'The New Coke debacle had been a very painful period for the business and it took some years to recover.

However, in the mid-1990s, under the recently re-appointed Chief Marketing Officer Sergio Zyman, Coke finally went back to basics and, rather than trying to fix its flat sales trends with promotions, initiatives and retailer spending binges it turned to its core proposition and asked 'Why aren't people buying us any more . . . and what do we need to do to change this?'

The first fundamental was to restore focus on who our core target customers really were – our 'Growth Sweet Spot' if you like. Under the pressure Pepsi had applied over recent years we had got dragged away from our core family consumers into competing with Pepsi for the youth market.

Crucial step number 1 was recognising that this younger market was not the 'Sweet Spot' for Coke. Almost by definition, because the brand had become adopted by 'Middle America' young people were likely to lean towards rejecting Coke in favour of a relative 'challenger' brand like Pepsi. Trying to compete with this group of consumers was competing on Pepsi's territory – they were always likely to have the upper hand.

Rather, we had to remind ourselves that we actually already 'owned' a huge slice of the market – middle American families – and that our best growth opportunity lay with them.

Once we had re-focused against this 'Sweet Spot' group we had to ask ourselves 'How did we build our autopilot status with this group originally – and how can we restore this?'

The answer came from examining Coke's history. In its strongest periods Coke had been the brand associated with social occasions – from meals with friends and family to bigger formal parties and celebrations. Famously, Coke had virtually re-branded Father Christmas in its red and white brand colours, and for many years, Coke Christmas advertising had signaled the start of the festive season.

We realised that we needed to re-connect with our Sweet Spot customers by re-claiming our association with the social occasions that mattered most to them. That meant focusing particularly on families – and therefore mums – as our core target group, and re-establishing Coke as the natural accompaniment to great times with the family or with friends.

Part of this repositioning work involved advertising, of course. So we took Coke back to its positioning as the drink to enjoy while sharing great times with family and friends.

We changed our approach to sports from a focus on the 'mean, edgy elite athletes' that Pepsi used to positioning Coke as the drink for sports fans – drink Coke while watching the big game with your friends. Remember 'Eat Football, Sleep Football, Drink Coca Cola'?

We re-energised our marketing around Christmas because of its importance as a family occasion. But not just Christmas – as we took our strategy around the world we made Coke the drink for sharing at other important festivals like Ramadan and Eid.

We re-thought our approach to packaging and re-introduced fridge packs so that sharing with the family would be easier than ever. Never a bad thing from a sales point of view either to have a 10-pack of Coke in the family fridge!

And this new approach to positioning led us to some great innovative ideas like printing names on our Coke bottles so that you could personalise the experience of sharing Coke with friends.

This re-positioning against the social occasions that meant most to our key target family consumers enabled us to re-establish the emotional connection that we had lost. And, once this was re-established, suddenly this group restored our 'permission to sell' and began responding once again to our advertising and our promotions.

And, after so many years where it had been very hard for Coke to grow, this repositioning delivered fantastic results very quickly. Over the 1993–1998 period Coke built its case sales from 10bn to 15bn units – even for a company as large and successful as Coke these were results worth celebrating!

And a great example, of course, of the impact of focusing clearly against the right target customer group, and then developing and implementing a proposition that connects emotionally with their lives.'

So – that's the first fundamental to becoming the default autopilot for your target customers: find a way to connect your brand with the emotional drivers of the dominant motivational goals in your category. Establishing that emotional connection is vital. Without it, you will not become the default autopilot in your chosen category.

Sometimes, simply being the brand that best establishes this connection is enough of a differentiator and can be enough to transform your propensity to become the default autopilot choice – the Dove example above illustrates this very well.

A Differentiated Performance Promise

In most cases you need to go further if you want to secure autopilot status. Beyond establishing this emotional connection and securing 'permission to sell', you need to make your target consumers a *differentiated performance promise* that is (i) different from/better than that offered by other brands, (ii) connects meaningfully with the emotional goal drivers of choice, and (iii) reinforced by usage of your brand. If you get this right, then you will be in position to secure autopilot status – and to grow.

So – what do I mean by this? Is it just a question of a simple functional promise like 'washes 5% whiter' or 'lasts 10% longer'? Well – not really.

Remember, autopilot status is secured by persuading the subconscious that your brand will enable fulfilment of the dominant emotional goals better than all others. This connection will usually initially be established through conventional marketing communications of one sort or another. But, once a brand has been chosen, the consumers' experience of the brand will become the key determinant of whether it establishes and retains autopilot status or whether it is trialled and then discarded. So – to become the default autopilot you must be able to make, and deliver, a performance promise that is differentiated from competitors, that connects meaningfully with the emotional goal drivers of category choice, and which you are confident will be reinforced by repeated usage.

The Growth Director says:
To secure autopilot status you need to offer a differentiated performance promise that beats others.

- A differentiated performance promise should use Insights to connect meaningfully with the emotional drivers of brand choice.
- A differentiated performance promise must offer performance/emotional reward that is different from/better than other brands.
- A differentiated performance promise must be believable in the context of your brand's reputation/equity and must be reinforced by usage.
- Sometimes (like the Dove Campaign for 'Real Beauty') a performance promise can be purely emotional.
- Often (Premier Inn is a good example) a differentiated performance promise will combine both emotional and functional elements.

To go back to the Felix example described above, Nestlé Purina understood that the key emotional goal drivers in the category were related to the desire of cat owners to secure expressions of love/affection from their cats. Connecting its brand with these emotional drivers was the key to securing a permission to sell from their target consumers that was denied to other brands.

In essence, the proposition was 'buy Felix and secure love and affection from your cat'. Crucially, this proposition was backed up, and then repeatedly reinforced, by the products Felix brought to market. Felix invested in their product formulas so that they had food flavours and varieties that cats actively preferred. This meant that usage of their products consistently produced the moments of affection that cat owners craved. Had their food been less well received than other brands then their proposition would have been undermined by repeated usage – and would probably have failed.

Building on their insight, Nestlé Purina also developed a sub-category of 'cat treat' food products. Now well established and of significant size, this category was an innovation at the time – but again enabled the Felix brand to connect very powerfully with the emotional goal drivers – cats came to crave the cat treat products; owners giving the treats were rewarded with affection – autopilot status reinforced!

So – a differentiated performance promise of direct relevance to the emotional goal drivers in the category and reinforced by product usage. The perfect combination.

A second useful example is a brand referred to elsewhere in this book – Premier Inn.

Premier Inn has achieved a strong leadership position in the budget hotels market by understanding that the key emotional driver behind choice of budget hotel is feeling confident that you will wake in the morning refreshed, energised and ready for the important business meeting/day out with friends that you have planned.

In itself, establishing this emotional connection would be an advantage to Premier Inn. But the brand has gone much further than this and has made itself a strong autopilot by developing and delivering a proposition which delivers on this insight in a differentiated and meaningful way, and which is reinforced with every Premier Inn visit.

To deliver on its 'wake up refreshed and energised' proposition Premier Inn has invested in much higher-quality mattresses than other budget hotels – in fact their mattresses are amongst the best of any hotels in the UK. In each Premier Inn bedroom there is a choice of four (yes – four!) different hardnesses of pillow – whatever your particular preference you will be able to find it. To reinforce their commitment to their 'wake up refreshed and energised' proposition, they have introduced a 'Good Night Guarantee', which they remind you of every time you make a booking or check in – if you do not get a good night's sleep (subject, of course, to certain terms and conditions!) the company will give you your money back. I've tried it – and they really do!

Of course, the Premier Inn advertising and marketing focuses very strongly on their 'wake up refreshed and energised' proposition –

reminding you of their commitment to this key goal every time you are exposed to one of their messages.

Has this worked? It certainly has. This is a beautiful example of a brand understanding the emotional goal drivers of its target consumers and developing a proposition that differentiates it from all other budget hotel brands, that connects meaningfully with the emotional goal drivers of choice in the category (waking up refreshed and energised) and that will be reinforced with every visit to a Premier Inn (not least by ensuring staff explain and offer the Good Night Guarantee on EVERY check-in interaction). It has driven spectacular success for the Premier Inn business.

Premier Inn now has a 40% share of the budget hotel category and has out-grown the market in each of the last five years – sustained, significant, profitable Good Growth.

One final example to show how important it is to get the differentiated performance promise exactly right for your target audience, concerns a malted drink called Milo which is a significant brand for Nestlé in Australia.

Using Milo, Nestlé had effectively built its own category and had a huge market share – around 85% of the malted milk market. Milo had been positioned as a fun drink for kids, and was seen by parents both as something their children enjoyed drinking, and as a neat way to get them used to drinking more milk. Nestlé's problem, however, was that the category that they had created was in decline, with parents increasingly moving their children away from this 'old fashioned' product into the new generation of 'energy' drinks which were marketed as being good for young, energetic children.

Nestlé's solution was to find a way to re-position the Milo brand as providing a better type of 'slow-release' energy for children that contrasted positively with the 'boom then bust' energy associated with sugary kids drinks. This new positioning had a strong scientific basis, and proved highly successful.

The point that I want to make in this chapter, however, is the way that Nestlé worked out how to flex its differentiated performance promise to fit with the different emotional goal drivers of its different target consumer groups:

- For children from 'typical Aussie' western-style backgrounds, Nestlé promised that Milo's 'slow release energy' would ensure the kids were ready to give their best to after-school sports activities which have high emotional importance to many Aussie mums and dads.
- For children from South and East Asian backgrounds, Nestlé promised that Milo would provide better concentration levels for homework and study after school.
- For children from the Pacific Islands, Nestlé promised that Milo's slow-release energy would ensure that children were ready to have fun with friends and family when school was finished.

For each of these groups the basic product proposition was the same – Milo's scientifically supported ability to provide long-lasting 'slow-release' energy – but the performance promise that this quality delivered was flexed to ensure it connected meaningfully with the most important emotional goal drivers of each sub-group of target customers.

Once these positions were established, Nestlé was able to reinforce the scientific basis for its proposition in every piece of advertising, on every pack of Milo that they put into the market and through in-store display materials and associated messaging –ensuring that the emotional connections established with the subconscious brains of its consumers were reinforced every time the product was used.

Autopilot status established – and secured. And of course the results followed. This refined and suitably targeted proposition turned around the decline that the Milo brand had been suffering from and enabled it to reestablish significant, consistent growth.

Let's recap. The last two chapters have established the essential components of securing autopilot status for a brand:

1. You must *define the target consumers* with whom you want to become the default autopilot choice – and this is not as straightforward as you might think
2. You must *uncover a powerful insight* that enables you to make an emotional connection with these consumers to give you 'permission to sell' at the key moments of autopilot choice.
3. You must offer them a *differentiated performance promise* that both connects meaningfully with the emotional drivers behind the Moments

of Maximum Emotional Impact (MoMIs) when autopilot choices are made, and is believably different from/better than competitive brands.

We have looked at both the importance of being very clear about who your target customers are and the neuroscience-based research techniques increasingly available to enable you to do this with a high degree of certainty that you are making the right choices.

We have also looked at the two essential elements of securing autopilot status – establishing an emotional connection with your target customers and offering them a differentiated performance promise which connects to the emotional goals that drive autopilot choice.

Later in this book we will examine in some detail how to use these insights to produce commercial and marketing plans that will drive significant, sustained and profitable growth for your business.

But, before we do this, we need to drill down further into those key emotional goal drivers that are at the heart of every autopilot decision that your subconscious brain takes, and to examine the crucial moments when these emotions are at their height, when autopilot decisions are made, and which provide by far the most powerful positioning opportunities for your business and your brands.

This is the subject of Chapter 7.

The Growth Director's Summary

- In order to develop a proposition that will secure autopilot status you need to

  - establish an emotional connection with target customers to secure 'permission to sell'; and
  - offer a differentiated performance promise that connects with the emotional goal drivers of category purchasing and is perceived as different from/better than all competitors,

- Our subconscious brains hardwire us to ignore/resist rational sales messages: to overcome this, we must connect emotionally with target consumers and secure 'permission to sell'.

- The key to emotional connection is to present your brand in the context of 'insights': core consumer truths that reveal when/explain why your product's performance is of such emotional importance to consumers.
- Presenting your brand in the context of powerful insights will unlock consumers emotionally and secure their 'permission to sell'.
- The Dove 'Campaign for Real Beauty' is a great example of a marketing campaign built around a very powerful consumer insight – that the beauty goal of most women is not to look like a supermodel, but to feel happy and confident about themselves
- To be effective a differentiated performance promise must:

  - be different from/better than promises offered by other brands;
  - connect meaningfully with the emotional goal drivers of choice; and
  - be reinforced by usage of your brand.

- Behind Premier Inn's 'Wake up Wonderful' proposition is a great example of a highly effective differentiated performance promise that has delivered significant, sustained and profitable growth.

Chapter 7

Moments of Maximum Emotional Impact: Understanding the emotionally-important moments that are key to autopilot brand choice

We have established that the key to significant, sustained, profitable growth is becoming the default autopilot brand for your target customers.

We examined in Chapter 6 how, to become the autopilot choice, you need both to connect emotionally with the motivational goals driving purchase behaviour in your category, and to offer customers a differentiated performance promise that is connected to those goal drivers and is different from/better than those made by other brands.

This chapter takes that analysis further, to examine the crucial Moments of Maximum Emotional Impact (MoMIs) when the emotions driving category purchase behaviour are at their peak and to explain how identifying and owning these MoMIs is the most effective way to secure lasting autopilot status.

Let's start with a little more brain science.

What is it about the way that our brains work that means certain moments are disproportionately important to us emotionally – and therefore are the ultimate drivers of brand preference and autopilot choice?

Context matters – hugely

To explain this, let's start with explaining how the context in which we take a decision affects how our brains react to it. Context matters –

hugely. To repeat the very simple, but useful, example I mentioned in Chapter 3, look at the two small central squares in the diagrams below – are they the same shade of grey or are they different?

Figure 7.1

Of course, the squares are exactly the same shade of grey – but they look different to our eyes – the right hand one looks darker. That is, of course, because of the difference in background colours – the darker background on the left makes your subconscious brain 'see' the central square on the left as a lighter shade than the one on the right hand side which is set against a lighter background. This is a simple (and slightly cumbersome) example of the difference to your brain's evaluation of any situation that 'context' makes.

Remember, your subconscious brain is constantly trying to make choices that best enable you to meet the dominant emotional goals in any given situation. An essential part of this calculation involves assessing the context of any situation you are in and being prepared to make a different decision based on a different context.

So – if you are deciding whether or not to buy a Coke, contextual factors like – how thirsty are you right now; how hot is it today; how far might you have to go to find another place to get a drink – will all have an important impact on your willingness to make this purchase: in effect, to trade something you value (money) for a drink right now. Context is crucial.

This is a very simple example where the contextual influences are fairly obvious – we know whether or not we are thirsty; we know whether or not it is a hot day. We call these 'explicit' factors.

In most situations, though, the contextual influences are not obvious to us – we are not consciously aware of them. However, our subconcious brain, which is continuously scanning our environment for 'clues' which will help it direct us to the right course of action, will pick up all relevant contextual influences and use these to guide its decision making. We almost always miss this.

> As humans, we don't consciously perceive how the situation, the environment, influences our behavior. It is therefore easy to underestimate the power of context to influence decisions . . . it remains implicit.
>
> Barden (2013)

To move this analysis on a stage further – context does not just guide whether or not we decide to make a category purchase, it also determines which brand we choose to buy. So, to take another simple example: our choice of ice-cream brand on a hot day will be influenced by whether we are out with the children (maybe ice lollies to cool down); out on our own (maybe a 'Magnum' as a treat); at home with the family (perhaps a Wall's 'Soft Scoop' tub); or entertaining friends (maybe a selection of exotic flavours from Häagen Dazs or Ben and Jerry's).

All of the examples above, however, deal with contextual factors which are largely explicit – things like whether or not we are thirsty, whether the weather is hot or not, whether we are buying for ourselves, or for our children, or for the family.

But most contextual factors are not explicit. They are factors linked to the emotional goals which drive our behaviours – and are therefore much more powerful in determining our course of action or, indeed, our choice of brands. We are mostly unaware of the influence of these implicit factors – but our subconscious brain always picks them up and factors them in to our decision-making and choice of brands – usually as the dominant influence.

Again, to take a simple example: a young man out drinking with a new group of friends might choose a 'blokey' beer like Fosters or Carlsberg to signal his 'mateship' with them; out with a group of older work colleagues, he might choose a regional bitter to signal maturity and 'depth'; out on a first date, he might choose a stylish continental bottled lager to signal sophistication and affluence.

The Growth Director says:
Context matters – hugely!

- Context makes a huge difference to how our brains react to situations and take decisions: 'Purchase decisions are determined by the situational context as this shapes the perceived value and costs' (Barden (2013)).
- Contextual factors can be explicit (like the effect on ice-cream purchasing of temperature) or implicit (such as the different social pressure you feel from, say, a work group compared to your family).
- Implicit factors are much more important than explicit ones in driving brand choice.
- Our subconscious brains make autopilot brand choices according to the perceived fit with the most emotionally important situations we are likely to encounter in any given product category.
- We tend to choose only the brand likely to best fit the needs of the most emotionally important situation we are likely to encounter. This is the 'Winner Takes All' effect and helps explain autopilot purchasing behaviour.

So what's the point of this? How is context important to understanding how to best position your brands to become the default autopilot choice?

Well, as we have seen in previous chapters, the key to becoming the default autopilot is to connect your brand most powerfully with the emotional goals driving category purchase decisions, and to provide a differentiated performance promise relevant to achievement of those goals. If you can do this, the subconscious brain of the consumers whose purchasing choice is driven by these goals will automatically choose you over other brands.

In deciding which brand best enables it to meet the dominant emotional goals, your subconscious brain will be acutely aware of all the situations for which these emotional goals are relevant. Within this, it will also understand which of these situations is the most important – or perhaps the one in which it is most difficult to satisfy the key emotional goals.

Your subconscious System 1 brain will most value the brand that is best able to satisfy the dominant emotional goals in the situations where this is most important/most difficult to achieve. Even though those situations may not be relevant at the time that you make a purchase decision, your subconscious brain will be aware that these situations are likely to occur at some point in the future and so will make a brand choice to ensure you have the best chance of coping with those situations when they occur.

In effect, your subconscious brain is making autopilot choices based on its evaluation of the most important usage occasion you are likely to face. So – if you can identify those situations – or moments – and position your brand to 'own' them, then you are most likely to become the default autopilot choice.

Importantly, this also helps to further explain our autopilot purchasing behaviour. Even if at the time we are making a purchase our situation is such that any one of a number of brands could 'satisfy' us, our subconscious brains are thinking ahead to the time when satisfaction of the dominant emotional goals is most important/most difficult, and will drive us to choose, time and time again, the brand that we have decided best enables us to meet these goals at these important moments.

Neuroscientists refer to this as 'The Winner Takes All Effect'. Only the brand that is at the top of our subconscious ranking for satisfaction of the dominant emotional goals will be chosen – just getting your brand in the consideration set is not good enough. Once this ranking is established, as we have seen in previous chapters, the subconscious System 1 brain is a very stubborn beast and is reluctant to re-evaluate its decision. Hence, autopilot shopping behaviour.

MoMIs

It's very important to ensure I have adequately made the distinction between a broad Emotional Goal Territory and a super-powerful 'Moment of Maximum Emotional Impact' – or 'MoMI'.

Brands that position themselves to connect with the emotional drivers of the dominant Emotional Goal Territory are doing the right thing and will probably have a degree of success. But brands that understand and 'own' the moments within those territories where emotional goal delivery is most important – or most difficult to achieve – will be the ones that secure autopilot status.

Let's use a couple of simple examples to illustrate this.

The first goes back a number of years – but is still a great example of this crucial distinction. The brand is 'Head & Shoulders' the anti-dandruff shampoo manufactured by Procter and Gamble.

Head & Shoulders built its business on understanding that dandruff was socially embarrassing and that a proposition based on eliminating it so that consumers could feel relaxed about their appearance in social situations was likely to occupy the Emotional Goal Territory in the shampoo market. For many years, both its positioning and its advertising concentrated on this broad territory of 'confidence in social situations' and the brand built a good business. However, over the years, other brands mimicking this positioning entered the market and Head & Shoulders' business flattened out.

Its breakthrough, however, came when it identified the relevant MoMI in this goal territory. The team discovered that the MoMI when the emotions around social confidence/embarrassment were most acute was when you were meeting an important new person for the first time – perhaps a new boss or important colleague at work; perhaps an attractive member of the opposite sex; perhaps just a social occasion like a party where you would be inevitably meeting new people you wanted to impress.

The Head & Shoulders team found that the emotional resonance of these occasions was much more powerful than all the other social situations that it had been showing in its advertising and marketing over the years – it had found its MoMI. Based on this insight, the brand developed a campaign built around the wonderfully powerful advertising slogan:

'You never get a Second Chance to make a First Impression.' Instant MoMI ownership.

This had immediate and significant impact on the brand's growth and took Head & Shoulders to an unassailable leadership position which it held (while continuing to run this campaign) for many years.

Simply, the importance of being able to deliver the emotional goal of confidence in a dandruff-free appearance was significantly enhanced at the moments when you were meeting an important new person with whom you wanted to create a good first impression. By understanding the superior power of this MoMI versus all other ways of connecting with the Emotional Goal Territory of social confidence, the brand reclaimed its autopilot status and baked-in significant growth trends for years to come.

For another example of the power of MoMIs to enable a brand to own an Emotional Goal Territory and become the default autopilot let me hand over to Stef Calcraft, founding partner of the 'Mother' advertising agency, who have been responsible for the Boots advertising campaigns of the last 10 years or so.

Case Study: Here Come The Girls – How Owning Powerful Moments Transformed Boots' Beauty Business; *by Stef Calcraft, Founding Partner, Mother Advertising Agency*

'Back in the mid 2000s Boots was struggling against the growing power of the big supermarkets in the Health and Beauty category. We were losing share and knew we had to re-establish the brand's credentials as being the place to go (the autopilot choice) for both healthcare services and beauty products and advice.

We wanted Boots to be seen as the place to come both for the best beauty products, but also for the advice that would ensure you chose the regime that was right for you – but in order to do this we had to find a way to connect Boots to the underlying – quite complex -emotional goals that lie behind the beauty regimes of most women.

We found an incredibly emotionally important moment which resonated really powerfully with women of all ages and which, when we connected Boots with it, enabled us to 'own' the relevant Emotional Goal Territory and reclaim Boots' position as the default autopilot destination for Beauty products.

The moment was related to perhaps the most important celebration we enjoy each year – Christmas. Christmas is an incredibly emotionally powerful time for all of us – and for women there is quite a complex cocktail of emotions at work.

An important component of the emotions associated with Christmas for many women is their desire to 'create' a wonderful celebration for those around them. In many families/couples it is the woman who takes the primary role in selecting and buying presents, preparing for the big day itself, and then cooking and serving the much-anticipated Christmas dinner. A large part of the emotional 'kick' she gets at Christmas is from the joy she's helped others to feel.

But there's another very important side to the emotions that women feel at Christmas – as well as being a time to facilitate the enjoyment of others – its also a time when she wants to party! And, as part of that she wants to be able to dress up, make up, and feel (and be told by others) that she's 'looking gorgeous'.

We chose a time when this desire is at its height – getting ready for the office Christmas party. Most women can empathise with this moment – there's a real competitive desire to look better than your workmates – and to attract the attention of the good looking guy from marketing. But it's also a real female bonding moment – helping each other get ready, admiring each others' dresses, and then sharing that huge adrenaline high as you and your girlfriends hit the party together.

We aimed to 'own' this moment for Boots by making an advertisement that captured, with both humour and real insight, this highlight of the beauty year. Our ad started in the office, showing women beginning to surreptitiously prepare for the party (when they should really have been working); extended to 'team' hair-styling and mass make-up sessions in the office toilets; and ended with the triumphant entrance at the party itself by a huge group of fully made up women in glamorous party dresses all looking – absolutely gorgeous!

Of course, as we let this story unfold we were able to showcase a range of Boots beauty products all selected to help its customers feel as gorgeous as the women in the ad. Importantly, the women in the ad were ' normal' women – all ages, all shapes and sizes. We wanted to say that we understood the desire of every woman to look and feel gorgeous from time to time – not just the few who looked like supermodels.

But the key to success of the advertising campaign – and indeed to the growth in Boots' beauty business over the next few years – was the song that we used as the soundtrack to this ad – a little-known track by an obscure '70s soul artist called Ernie K Doe. The track was 'Here Come The Girls' – and it became not only the theme of our Boots beauty advertising but an anthem for women everywhere wanting to glam up, look gorgeous and go out to party!

The music track, and the celebratory, humorous tone of the ad perfectly captured the emotions that lie behind why looking gorgeous at Christmas (and other times) is so important to most women. It's not just about attracting the opposite sex – it's also about bonding with your girlfriends and having a great time together.

By showing that Boots understood these emotions, and that because of this was providing the products and expert advice women needed to look and feel gorgeous, Boots was able to grab ownership of the moments when looking great is most important – and that gave them a route to 'auto-pilot' status in the beauty products market for many women. Its Christmas ad tag-line 'Tis The Season To Be Gorgeous' summed this up perfectly – and resonated hugely powerfully with women across the UK.

We followed this ad with a number of others in the same vein, focusing on other moments when looking gorgeous has high emotional importance (for example that first day of the summer holiday on the beach), and all using the 'Here Come The Girls' theme that evoked the emotions behind those moments.

The campaign, together with Boots' wonderful range of products, expert advice and improved shopping environments in its stores enabled the business to reclaim ownership of the beauty category for women across the UK and drove strong market share, sales and profit growth over a number of years.'

I hope that the difference between a broad Emotional Goal Territory and the very specific Moments of Maximum Emotional Impact (MoMIs) that most powerfully activate those moments is clear, and that the case for how 'ownership' of these MoMIs is the most effective way to secure autopilot status has also been made effectively.

In the box below, I have included some other illustrative examples of how powerful connecting with these MoMIs can be – once the concept is understood you can see how many of the most powerful brands have achieved their success by finding ways to own these moments in their business categories.

Brands, Emotional Goal Territories and MOMIs: Some Examples

- Brand: Head & Shoulders; Emotional Goal Territory: Social confidence; MoMI: First opportunity to make an impression with potentially important person.
- Brand: Premier Inn; Emotional Goal Territory: Confidence in having a comfortable night's sleep; MoMI: Moment of waking up refreshed and reenergised.
- Brand: John Lewis Christmas campaign; Emotional Goal Territory: Satisfaction of giving great presents at Christmas; MoMI: Moment when recipient reacts emotionally to your gift (tears from the Old Man in the Moon).
- Brand: MoneySupermarket; Emotional Goal Territory: Relief of securing cheaper car insurance; MoMI: Celebratory demonstration of the confidence that relief brings ('X saved money on his car insurance – and now he feels Epic!')
- Brand: Asda; Emotional Goal Territory: Confidence in securing best value shopping; MoMI: Moment of leaving the check-out with more money in your pocket than expected (the 'pocket tap' at the end of ads).

So – what are the implications of this phenomenon for approaching the task of positioning brands to achieve significant, sustained, profitable growth? Does this mean, in particular, that the MoMIs need to be shown explicitly in the marketing and advertising of brands that aspire to autopilot status?

Well – not necessarily – it rather depends on the characteristics of a product category.

There are some categories where the emotions behind a MoMI are so particular to that set of circumstances that the best way to evoke them is to target the moment very directly. I'll look at examples of this in a moment. In many categories, though, because the emotions behind the key MoMIs are so powerful, consumers will recognise them even when they are not in that situation themselves. This is fortunate for the development of many marketing and advertising campaigns!

Let's look at an example of each of these circumstances.

Banking

First, an example of where interacting with consumers at the identified MoMI itself is key to building emotional connection and securing autopilot status. For this I turn to the Financial Services sector.

When I worked as CMO at Barclay's Bank (for the Retail and Business Banking Division) customer satisfaction with all banks was very low. This was in the immediate aftermath of the financial crash for which the banks took much popular blame, but was also particularly directed at Barclays since the bank had been heavily and publicly criticized for matters such as attempting to manipulate the LIBOR inter-bank lending rate. It was a certainly a very tough time to be asked to rebuild the bank's reputation and its connection with its customers!

As a result of extensive consumer research we identified that the fundamental consumer issue with banks was that dealings always felt hugely impersonal – the banks seemed to care little about the lives of their customers and seemed to regarded them primarily as 'account numbers' rather than people. Interactions were always conducted in a very transactional way (banks were very happy to provide you with a mortgage but seemed to care very little about whether you moved into your new house successfully), and dealings with banks were done on their terms. If you wanted to open a current account, banks would offer you the same three or four options that they offered everyone – there was no allowance made for the very different lives we all lead.

Our research told us that a proposition based around making banking feel less 'bank-shaped' and more 'flexibly shaped around each individual's particular needs' would be very unexpected – and would have powerful resonance with most customers. We called this approach 'You-Shaped Banking'.

Behind the 'You-Shaped Banking' strategy we began to introduce innovative ideas that were designed to address the individual flexibility consumers wanted – innovations like introducing money transfers via mobile phones (the 'PingIt' initiative); offering current accounts that could be built individually to suit each person's particular needs – like selecting apps from the Apple App Store (we called it 'The Features Store'); allowing customers to personalise their debit cards with any picture of their choice (their pet/their partner/their football team etc) rather than the bank's logo.

All of these initiatives were successful in their own right – and began to rebuild the bank's reputation. But they still lacked the powerful emotional connection needed to establish autopilot status for Barclays.

To achieve this we had to recognise that, of all the many interactions a customer ever has with its bank, most are routine in nature and their emotional resonance is limited. There are, however, a small number of interactions which have very high emotional importance to the customer – and it is at these moments that they most want to feel they are being treated as individuals.

What are these Banking MoMIs? Well – we spent a lot of time, and a lot of research money attempting to find this out. As the results of this work emerged it became very clear that the banking MoMIs are occasions when the financial interactions have particular emotional impact in customers' lives – occasions like securing a mortgage (which in effect means securing a family home), asking for a loan (in itself an emotionally challenging thing to do – 'what if I get turned down?') or making important investment decisions related to pension planning (securing your future).

We identified a small number of these 'Banking MoMIs' and realised that, to secure autopilot status we had to bring 'You-Shaped Banking' solutions to these occasions – our strategy just would not have the same emotional resonance elsewhere (and therefore would not have the same power to drive autopilot choice).

We did this through initiatives like introducing new types of mortgage where parents/grandparents could fund mortgage deposits for their children without losing any interest on their savings (its called the

'Family Springboard Mortgage' – a great innovation) – and a range of other 'You-Shaped' ideas.

The point is, in this sector, the full impact of the MoMIs could ONLY be felt at the moments that they occurred. If you were not in the situation of having a child unable to afford a deposit for their first house then the emotions involved were not relevant to you; if you were in this situation, the emotions were hugely powerful and the bank that understood this and provided a solution would differentiate itself from all others and quickly become your autopilot choice for all financial transactions – not just this specific one.

So – in some sectors, like banks, the emotions that you need to own are only truly felt when those powerful MoMIs occur – and your proposition needs to reflect this by targeting those moments very specifically. The Scottish Rugby case study later in this chapter is another great illustration of how powerful MoMIs sometimes need to be evoked when they are most relevant (in the case of rugby, around the time when international matches are about to happen).

Not many sectors are like this though. In most cases, the emotions behind the category MoMIs are so commonly experienced, and so powerfully felt by category consumers that they can be evoked at any time and will trigger an emotional connection even if the consumer is not experiencing the MoMI at that point.

There are many examples of brands that have become successful by owning MoMIs that are recognised by all category consumers and will trigger autopilot behaviour whether the consumer is experiencing the MoMI or not. Examples like Lynx, which evokes the powerful emotions for young men around the moment they meet attractive girls; or Head & Shoulders which evokes the underlying worry we all have of making a bad first impression with an important person; or the well-known Asda 'pocket tap' campaign which evokes the pleasure and satisfaction of spending less at the supermarket checkout than you had expected to.

But – whether the MoMI requires the consumer to be actually experiencing it for full impact, or whether (as happens more commonly) it can be evoked by a brand with the right insight and understanding, these moments are the key to securing autopilot status. Our subconcious brains are acutely aware of these moments and their importance to us and are continually scanning the environment to find the brands that will best enable us to satisfy the emotional goals that these MoMIs most powerfully activate.

An understanding that identifying and owning the key MoMIs in your category should be at the heart of any brand's growth strategy – this understanding should drive proposition development ('have I got a proposition that will resonate stronger than all others at those key MoMIs?'); execution of that proposition ('are the key emotional and performance edges clear and easy for consumers to see and experience?'); and, importantly, marketing planning and execution.

The Growth Director says:
Understanding MoMIs is the key to securing autopilot choice

- Moments of Maximum Emotional Impact are those moments when the emotions driving choice in the category are at their most intense.
- Autopilot decisions are made at these MoMIs – to be chosen you must be perceived as the brand most likely to best deliver against the emotional drivers of choice in the most important contextual situation.
- Some MoMIs can only be connected with when the consumer is experiencing them. An example would be a bank seeking to connect with consumers looking for a mortgage to buy a house.
- In many cases MoMIs can be evoked so that autopilot choices will be made even if the consumer is experiencing the moment. An example would be the Head & Shoulders campaign evoking moments when you meet an important person for the first time.
- Out-performance at MoMIs should drive all elements of your commercial proposition – NOT just your marketing plans.

A particular challenge for marketing directors, advertising and media agencies everywhere is to approach consumer targeting not by the traditional method of aiming for particular socio-demographic sets ('young males aged 25–40 from social classes C1, C2 earning between £25,000 and £40,000 annually and living in London and the south-east' ... etc ...) but rather by targeting moments and the emotional goal drivers that lie behind them. This is a big challenge for conventional marketing thinking and we will address it in subsequent chapters.

Having established the crucial importance of owning MoMIs if you are to secure autopilot status – we need finally to cover the question 'How do you go about identifying what the MoMIs are?' As has been covered in previous chapters, identification of MoMIs poses a real challenge for conventional research. Traditional research techniques like Focus Groups, one-on-one Depth Interviews, online surveys, diary studies etc all interact primarily with our conscious System 2 brains which work predominantly in a rational manner. This poses quite a challenge in identifying and understanding MoMIs which are driven by emotional, not rational, factors, and which are embedded in our subconscious brains.

The best way to uncover these moments and the emotions behind them is to employ some of the new neuroscience-driven techniques emerging from the post-Kahneman understanding of our subconscious brains. Because these techniques are able to connect directly with our subconscious decision-making processes and because they are able to map the emotional goal drivers of purchase behaviour they are able to identify and understand the key MoMIs much more directly than conventional research.

It is not the purpose of this book to explain the various neuroscience-based research techniques that have emerged over recent years – but many now exist, ranging from laboratory-based tools that directly monitor brain activity to online 'implicit' tools that can connect with the subconscious by factoring in speed of response to stimuli as well as the responses given. These tools may not be suitable in all situations – but where they can be used they provide levels of insight that it is very hard to reproduce using conventional research methods.

However, not all companies are yet comfortable with these new tools and, for those that are not, there is no alternative to painstakingly getting close to the lives of your consumers, understanding and mapping the occasions when your products are used, and identifying through observation and interview the occasions when success or failure of a particular product or service is of disproportionate emotional importance to its users.

An important help with this task is to understand the influence of small groups of high-frequency 'Market-Making Customers' who exist in all categories and who can provide shortcuts to understanding the emotional drivers of purchase behaviour.

'Market-Making Customers' are the subject of Chapter 9, so I will not dwell on them here other than by explaining that, because these consumers are the highest-frequency/highest-volume users in any given category they:

- notice, and care more about product performance in any given category;
- are best able to reveal the moments when emotional engagement with product performance is greatest, and provide insights into the reasons for this;
- are typically very happy to talk about products/services in a category they use so frequently and therefore are 'fast' routes to insights/ identification of MoMIs; and
- are highly influential with other less frequent category users – setting the standards for performance expectation, influencing the views of others as to which brands are the best, and, by their 'ownership' of a large proportion of category sales, having a significant impact on retailers/distributors and the brands they favour.

Diligent observation and skillful interaction with these consumers is the fastest 'conventional' way to get to the emotional insights behind each category and to identify the MoMIs that drive brand choice. Chapter 9 discusses these consumers, their influence on a category, the insights that they can bring and, importantly, their potential impact on wider consumer attitudes towards the brands in that category.

But – either through use of neuroscience-based techniques (which I strongly recommend) or through diligent mapping and observation of 'Market-Making' consumer usage and reaction to your products, MoMIs can be identified. If you are to develop propositions that will reliably deliver autopilot status and significant, sustained, profitable growth, then they must be.

So – we have established over the last two chapters the essential emotional components of developing an autopilot proposition:

1. *Uncovering of a powerful emotional insight*: A core consumer truth which explains when and why your product's/service's performance is of emotional importance to your consumers. Presenting your product in the context of a powerful Insight will enable you to 'unlock' consumers emotionally and will provide you with 'permission to sell' to them.
2. *Identification of the 'Moments of Maximum Emotional Impact'* ('MoMIs'): Those particular circumstances or times when the impact of the insight is at its most powerful.

If you can present your product or service in the context of these moments, and can offer consumers a *differentiated performance promise* that persuades them that your brand delivers against the emotional goals behind these moments better than your competitors, then you will get huge brand choice in your favour and will secure the autopilot status that is the basis for significant, sustained, profitable growth.

So – how is such a proposition developed, what are its key elements, and what impact is its development likely to have on your brand and your business?

These are the subjects of our next chapter.

Case Study: How Connection with MoMIs Drives Growth in Scottish Rugby; *by Phil Anderton, ex CEO Scottish Rugby*

Phil has worked in senior marketing positions in major companies all over the world, including five years at Procter and Gamble and seven years working for Coca-Cola (Coke) in the US and in Europe including a spell as Global Brand Manager in the 1990s.

Phil has also been Chief Marketing Officer of the ATP World Tour, has been CEO of Scottish Rugby and of Hearts Football Club, and has been CEO of Al Jazira in the Emirates.

When Phil joined Scottish Rugby, first as Marketing Director and then as CEO, the business was struggling to grow revenues. National interest in the team was mainly confined to rugby clubs and rugby enthusiasts; match-day revenues were static, and sponsorship funding was unimpressive.

Here's Phil's story of how an understanding of the key moments that could fire fans' enthusiasm and thus regenerate broader interest in the sport delivered substantial revenue growth.

'Scottish Rubgy, like many sports, had become overly focused on the experts – the players, the clubs and the administrators. It had lost sight of the most important group of all – certainly from a commercial point of view – the fans, without whose enthusiasm commercial progress would be very difficult to achieve.

Our first task was to challenge and re-define who we were building our business for – in effect who were our target 'Sweet Spot' customers. Traditionally, the focus had been Scottish rugby club members – they had made up most of the crowd on match day and they had influence with the committees who were highly influential in the administration of the game.

We came to quickly realize, however, that this was limiting our potential to grow. More importantly, it became clear that our over-focus on this group (where we had already saturated our commercial potential) had prevented us from seeing the opportunity with a much larger group – passionate Scots (and there are a lot of them!) for whom the national rugby team could become a focus of their patriotism. Incredibly, some of this group felt so excluded that they thought they would not be able to attend Scotland matches as attendance was restricted to rugby club members!

Attracting this much larger group meant reaching out beyond the tight-knit community of rugby club members to connect with families, mums and dads, school children etc all of whom had the potential to get excited by supporting the Scottish team.

But – how could we do this? How could we re-establish emotional connection with a group who had felt excluded for a long time?

The answer was to focus on match days as an exciting event, and a wonderful opportunity to celebrate Scottishness with family and friends. While this broadening of our approach to Scottish rugby was a huge step forward, the key to the success of what we did was understanding what the key moments were that could activate the intense passions shared by all proud Scots.

These moments were not the scoring of a try, a piece of brilliant skill on the pitch, even the high of an important victory. Our research told us that the key Moment of Maximum Emotional Impact for our 'passionate Scot' target consumer was for a dad, or a mum, arriving at the game with their son (or daughter) and experiencing with them a surge of shared pride in their Scottishness.

So – we built a proposition that would connect most powerfully with this moment. We built up the 'theatre' of match day itself – we had fireworks exploding over the stadium; a lone piper on the roof of Murrayfield before kick-off; a stirringly patriotic poem read out over the loudspeakers as the teams were about to emerge. All of this to give that dad/son or mum/daughter combination the opportunity to celebrate their pride in being Scottish.

We also took this 'moment' beyond the ground by scaling up our involvement with schools and local communities ahead of match days, encouraging sponsors to do likewise, and generally used the events of international matches as an opportunity for national celebration of our Scottishness.

An incredibly powerful moment. And our connection with this moment worked incredibly well. Attendances at matches leapt dramatically. Revenues went from £16m to £28m in three years. We even saw a significant increase in the numbers of people playing rugby regularly across Scotland.

Identifying those powerful moments and building a proposition tightly focused around them can have hugely positive impacts on your business – in sport as in all other commercial areas.'

The Growth Director's Summary

- Context makes a huge difference to how our brains react to situations and take decisions – including purchasing decisions and brand choices.
- Contextual factors that affect decision making can be explicit (like the effect on ice-cream purchasing of the temperature) or implicit (the social pressure you feel from different groups – say friends, family, work colleagues).
- Implicit factors are usually more powerful in driving brand choice.

- Our subconcious brains choose brands according to their perceived fit with the most emotionally important situations we are likely to encounter in any given product category.
- We will choose only the top-ranked brand – being ranked second-best is worthless. This is called the 'Winner Takes All Effect' and helps explain autopilot purchasing behaviour.
- Within each Emotional Goal Territory are key moments when the emotions driving brand choice are at their most intense. We call these 'Moments of Maximum Emotional Impact' or 'MoMIs'.
- Key to autopilot selection is being perceived as most likely to meet the needs of the key category MoMIs.
- Some MoMIs (such as in banking) can only be connected with when the consumer is experiencing the moment 'for real'; in many cases, MoMIs can be evoked – this is the key to successful positioning and marketing.
- Out-performance at MoMIs should drive all elements of your brand's commercial proposition – not just its marketing.

Chapter 8

Building a Catnip Proposition: How to build a proposition that will secure autopilot status for your brand

If you own a cat you probably know about catnip. For those of you who have never managed to acquire a feline companion, here are just two of the many online descriptions of what catnip does to otherwise peaceful cats:

> Catnip drives felines crazy, causing them to roll around on the floor and paw at invisible birds flying in their vicinity.

> Owner's descriptions of the effects of catnip on their pets range from arousal to euphoria to sedation, with some cats drooling during exposure.

Sounds like fun!! Catnip is another name for the herb Nepeta Cataria, which is a relatively common roadside plant in many parts of the northern hemisphere, and is related to oregano and spearmint (so the internet tells me . . .). Catnip contains nepetalactone, a molecule which scientists believe mimics a cat pheromone. Whatever the chemistry, anyone who has given their cat a product containing catnip will know how irresistible they find it – it literally drives them temporarily crazy!

It is not the intention of this book to show businesses how to reproduce drug-induced euphoria in their customers – but we do intend to explain how to develop brand propositions that are as compelling and attractive in their own way to target customers as catnip is to cats.

The 'Catnip Proposition'

A 'Catnip Proposition' is how we describe something that is so compelling for customers that it enables the brand concerned to secure autopilot status in its category and hence to achieve significant, sustained, profitable growth. In the same way that cats do not consciously choose to be affected by the catnip herb, a successful Catnip Proposition will connect powerfully with the emotional drivers of brand choice and elicit a subconscious decision to purchase. Not quite 'driving your consumers wild with desire' – but the closest commercial equivalent!

Let's briefly recap the key pieces of thinking that have got us to this point in our growth journey and help to underline the importance of understanding how to build a Catnip Proposition for your business.

- The only type of growth worth having is what we call 'Good Growth' – growth driven by developing propositions that are so compelling that they will recruit customers month-by-month and year-by-year but without the need for excessive (and profit-destroying) pricing/promotional/initiative-driven activity.
- Although almost all companies would agree that this is the type of growth they crave, the statistics show that most are really bad at delivering it. To take just one example that we discussed earlier, Bain & Co data from 2012/13 suggests that nine out of 10 management teams fail to grow their companies profitably. We call this *the Growth Paradox*.
- The most important reason for The Growth Paradox is that most companies make a common *Big Growth Mistake* – making the assumption that all consumer purchases are potentially available to them, and building super-busy commercial plans that seek to grab as many of these as possible. This is expensive, wasteful and usually fails to deliver sustainable, profitable growth.
- The *Growth Secret* that most companies miss is that most of the time we shop on 'autopilot' from a small portfolio of favourite brands – in most categories our autopilot brands account for 75–90% of all the purchases we make. Because our brains have hard-wired us to select our autopilot favourites with minimal effort, we fail to notice most attempts by competing brands to attract our attention. Hence the huge waste endemic in most commercial plans.
- The key to Good Growth is learning how to become the dominant autopilot brand in your category – that's it. But this is tough. Autopilot choices are made subconsciously at a small number of emotionally-important 'Moments of Maximum Emotional Impact'

(MoMIs). Because they are made subconsciously and are emotionally driven, our conscious brains are mostly unaware of when or why we make these decisions – so they remain almost undetectable by conventional research methods.

- To become the default autopilot brand in your category you need to understand three things: (i) With *which consumers* do you have the best chance of becoming the default auto-pilot? (ii) How do you establish an *emotional connection* with these consumers so that they grant you 'permission to sell'? (iii) What is the *differentiated performance promise* that you can credibly offer them to secure preference at the key Moments of Maximum Emotional Impact and hence autopilot status?

Let us assume that all this has been understood by your business and that you have identified a group of target consumers who are big enough to deliver the growth you need and with whom you have a fighting chance of securing autopilot status. You now need to combine the insights you have uncovered about your target consumers' lives, the moments when autopilot decisions are made and the emotions behind these moments with a deliverable performance promise that will both be credible for your brand to make and will secure preference at those key MoMIs.

You need, in effect, to develop a Catnip Proposition.

It is very important not to think of developing a Catnip Proposition – and writing it down – as either an academic exercise or as something with relevance only for the marketing department. For a Catnip Proposition to secure autopilot status for your brand/business and thus to deliver significant, sustained, profitable growth, *it must become the key focus for commercial activity across your organisation*. That means your Catnip Proposition should:

- drive product and packaging development priorities
- determine your approach to pricing
- enable you to understand the cost structure your business needs to deliver sustainable, profitable growth
- have an important influence on your distribution strategy and priorities
- drive all your marketing and promotional activity
- direct media planning and guide all creative advertising development

- be the dominant influence as you decide how to allocate your company's commercial resources.

If your Catnip Proposition is to deliver the impact in the market that you intend, it must be understood and 'bought into' across your business. You need to focus on its delivery and to have metrics in place to tell you whether or not you are doing this effectively. The best and most successful businesses will have a very clear understanding of their proposition – employees across the business would be able to describe it, understand why its delivery is so important, and know what role they are personally playing in its delivery.

Later in this chapter we will examine some well-known examples of companies who have this clarity – and who have achieved spectacular growth results as a consequence. Before we get into these examples, though, let us review the components of an effective Catnip Proposition. It has the following essential elements:

(i)   it makes very clear which consumers (or consumer mind-sets) it is targeting – in essence, the consumers (or mind-sets) it aims to become the autopilot choice for. Catnip Propositions are, by their nature, highly selective – they are compellingly appealing to their target customers, but may well have little appeal beyond that group (catnip drives cats wild . . . doesn't do much for dogs!);

(ii) it is explicit about the MoMIs that it is seeking to influence and it connects directly with the emotions behind this MoMI; and

(iii) it makes a clear 'differentiated performance promise' that, if delivered, will secure preference at the identified MoMI.

Our strong advice is that, as companies go about developing a Catnip Proposition that will secure autopilot status, they formalise it and write it down. The clarity that a formal statement brings, and the consistent reference point it provides can make a significant difference to facilitating the organisational focus against the drivers of growth that (as we pointed out in Chapter 1) so many companies lack. The format for this written statement can differ with every company that uses it. However, the three essential components outlined above must be present if the business is to turn a theoretically powerful proposition into commercial activity that drives significant, sustained, profitable growth.

The Growth Director says:
Catnip Propositions – designed to drive your customers wild!

- A Catnip Proposition is a commercial offering that is so irresistible to target consumers that, if delivered, it will secure autopilot status for your brand.
- The key elements of a Catnip Proposition are:

    - it makes clear which consumers/consumer mind-sets it is targeting – and it is happy to de-prioritise others; and
    - it is explicit about the MoMIs it is seeking to connect with and the emotions behind them
    - it is clear about the differentiated performance promise it is making.

- A Catnip Proposition must drive all commercial activity across your business – it is NOT just something for the marketing department.
- Employees across the business must be familiar with understand your Catnip Proposition – it should be everyone's mission to help deliver it.

The Catnip Proposition in practice

That's enough theory. Let's look at some businesses that have developed and brought to market effective Catnip Propositions and have achieved significant growth results as a consequence.

To begin with I want to return to two businesses we have looked at previously – Premier Inn and Uber. Both these organisations, in different ways and in very different markets, show how businesses that are driven by Catnip Propositions will deliver significant, sustained and profitable growth.

Premier Inn

The business is very clear about its target market. It makes no attempt to sell itself to consumers looking for an upmarket, leisure-driven hotel experience. It does not try to offer rooms with generously stocked mini bars (in fact there are no mini bars); it does not provide luxurious (or indeed any) fluffy dressing gowns for guests; it does not offer swimming pools, spas or even a gym; and it spends very little time trying to persuade customers to spend extended holiday periods in its hotels.

Rather, Premier Inn understands that other (more expensive) chains will cater for these occasions much more effectively. Instead, it focuses its appeal, its proposition and its marketing efforts on travellers looking for a one- or two-night stay, usually in city centre locations, where low unit price is a high priority. That brings its focus onto business people travelling to attend meetings, and middle-to-low income consumers looking for a short city-centre stay.

Notably, while some of these consumers may well stay at more luxurious (and more expensive) hotels at other times, Premier Inn understands it is targeting these individuals on those occasions when they are in a mind-set where low price/good value is an important driver of choice.

Having clarified its target consumers, Premier Inn has also done a great job of understanding the key MoMIs when autopilot decisions are made. Unlike other budget hotel chains, Premier Inn does not attempt to sell itself as a slightly down-market version of a luxury hotel – rather it has understood that, when choosing to stay in a budget hotel, consumers have very different priorities.

The key insight is that, unlike with more up-market hotels, staying at a Premier Inn is usually driven by functional rather than leisure needs. By far the most important of these needs is to wake in the morning feeling refreshed, energised and ready for the day's challenges.

For businessmen, that challenge might be an important meeting; for non-business travellers it might be a day out in the city or shopping with friends. In both cases, the key requirement, and the moment that will ultimately determine whether or not the stay has been successful is whether the customer wakes in the morning refreshed, energised and ready for a great day ... or tired, grumpy and wishing they could go back to sleep.

Having identified its target customers and understood the key moment that will determine the success or failure of their stay, Premier Inn has then crafted a proposition to ensure it delivers more effectively against this moment than any of its budget hotel rivals. By removing 'traditional' hotel features like minibars, fluffy dressing gowns, gym facilities and reducing its costs, it has been able to invest in the parts of its proposition that make the biggest impact at the identified MoMI. So – Premier Inn have some of the highest-quality mattresses of any hotel chain in the UK (Hypnos mattresses – you can even buy them on the Premier Inn website!); in each room they provide four pillows of varying degrees of hardness – so whatever your preference the chances are you'll sleep comfortably there; they have invested in good-quality duvets; and they offer all customers a 'Good Night Guarantee' – if you fail to have a good night's sleep then (subject, of course to terms and conditions!) they will offer you your money back. And they really do – I've tried it.

If I was trying to summarise the proposition that seems to be driving the Premier Inn commercial operation I might express it something like this:

> Premier Inn ensures busy travellers on a budget always wake up refreshed and energised. This is because Premier Inn understands the importance of a good night's sleep and so invest in mattresses, pillows and sheets all underpinned by the Good Night Guarantee.

Finally, their advertising and marketing, while far from the most creative or emotionally engaging, consistently focuses on bringing their identified MoMI to life – in the UK the advertising shows a refreshed Lenny Henry (the well-known comedian and actor) waking refreshed and energised in various unusual locations. The beautifully succinct campaign tag-line is 'Wake Up Wonderful'.

Since this proposition was adopted in 2008, the results have been spectacular. Premier Inn now has a share of the budget hotel market approaching 40% and have outgrown their category consistently in each of the past five years. A business built on a MoMI-driven, highly focused Catnip Proposition and delivering significant, sustained and profitable Good Growth.

This step-up in performance has not happened by chance. Just look at how well Premier Inn has delivered against the key ingredients of a Catnip Proposition:

- *Clear focus against defined target customers*: Tick.
  Business/leisure travellers looking for good value accommodation in/close to city centres

- *Identification of powerful Moments of Maximum Emotional Impact*: Tick. Waking up in the morning refreshed, energised and ready for a great day.
- *Development and delivery of proposition* to deliver against the drivers of that MoMI: Tick.
  Superior quality mattresses and duvets; choice of four pillow types; Good Night Guarantee. Savings made in other less important areas to pay for these investments.
- *Marketing that dramatises the proposition at the key MoMIs*: Tick.
  Lenny Henry's 'Wake Up Wonderful' TV campaign and associated on-line/off-line marketing all dramatise how Premier Inn understands the key moment and delivers against it.

Result? Autopilot status secured; sustained, profitable growth delivered.

Uber

Uber is the taxi-hire company that has come from nowhere to build a significant global business (and upset traditional taxi drivers everywhere) in just a few years.

Again, the Catnip Proposition elements are very clear.

Uber targets a consumer mind-set more than a socio-demographic group. Uber appeals to busy, tech-savvy consumers who like to be in control of their lives – while Uber skews towards young urban professionals, its appeal extends to many different consumer profiles when they are in 'I need a taxi – now!' mode.

Uber has understood that the dominant emotional goal is to stay in control of the process of finding a taxi and getting to your destination on time. For busy consumers in a hurry the great subconscious worry is being unable to find a suitable taxi when you need it. No-one likes standing in the street competing with other late-night or rush-hour travellers for the next passing cab. Everyone has had the experience of being told a mini-cab will be '5–7' minutes – only to be still waiting 25 minutes (and multiple angry follow-up phone calls) later. And most of us have also felt 'ripped off' by a taxi or mini-cab who, realising our predicament, has charged what seems like a hugely inflated rate for a short trip.

Uber has understood the emotional importance of the moment when you think 'I need a taxi – fast . . . but how easy will it be to find one?' –

and has developed a proposition to address this significantly better than all conventional alternatives.

By using its smartphone app, Uber users can choose the taxi that is closest to them; they will know exactly how far away their chosen taxi is; and they will have an indicative price quoted before they make their choice – all accessible via their smartphone from their bar stool or business meeting.

Uber's proposition addresses the emotional needs behind the moment when you realise you need a taxi by returning control of the process to the traveller. This is such a powerful motivator that, even if you might actually have found a taxi more quickly by hailing one in the street, or more cheaply by calling a minicab firm, Uber has become the autopilot for a huge group of high-frequency taxi users almost overnight. From a standing start in San Francisco in 2011, Uber now operates in 300 cities in 58 countries and is valued at over $60bn –which definitely counts as Good Growth.

If I was to draft a written Catnip Proposition for Uber it might look something like this:

> Uber ensures busy people can always be sure of securing a safe, reliable taxi quickly. This is because Uber understands the frustration of being unable to secure a taxi when you most need one and so uses smart phone technology to put a safe, reliable taxi just one click away.

This classic Catnip Proposition has secured autopilot choice amongst a core group of target customers which has in turn driven sustained (and in the case of Uber, spectacular) growth. As with Premier Inn, the Uber proposition and delivery ticks all the catnip boxes:

- *Clear focus against defined target customers*: Tick.
  Busy, tech savvy consumers who like to be in control of things.
- *Identification of powerful Moments of Maximum Emotional Impact*: Tick.
  Moment when you realise you need a taxi – fast – and worrying about whether you'll be able to get one.
- *Development and delivery of proposition* to deliver against the drivers of that MoMI: Tick.

Smartphone app puts consumer in control, allowing you to view and choose taxi options, plus receive fare estimate before booking.

- *Marketing that dramatises the proposition at the key MoMIs*: Tick.
Mainly through PR, plus the power of advocacy, Uber has made its proposition famous, fast.

The final example I want to cover in this section is a brand that has made a breakthrough impact in a very traditional sector by applying Catnip Proposition principles to deliver its appeal. The brand is the detergent brand Method, which has broken into the incredibly competitive US detergent market and is beginning to build share in international markets like the UK and Germany.

Method

For those of you not yet familiar with the Method range, I recommend you go online and take a look – Method products do not look or smell anything like conventional cleaning products. Method products are presented in super-cool, beautifully styled bottles in shapes like perfect tear-drops, or designs that evoke cosmetics more than floor cleaners. Packs are high-quality transparent plastic which enables the user to see the incredibly bright, almost candy-coloured products. And Method uses exotic perfumes like pomegranate, almond and eucaplytus mint– way more exciting than the category norms. Method says its products 'clean like heck and smell like heaven' and invits its users to 'Clean Happy' – not your average detergent brand!

As this should all make clear, Method is not a traditional cleaning product brand, but it has managed to build share against some of the most strongly entrenched brand franchises in one of the most conservative and risk-averse categories in the world by applying what are, in effect, Catnip Proposition principles.

Not only does Method look (and smell) very different from conventional cleaning products, it has also been developed to be substantially 'greener' (better for the environment) than most other detergent products. Method understood that, in a rather old-fashioned and functional category, its unconventional designs, bright product and packaging colours, high-impact perfumes and 'green credentials' could not only stand out, but more importantly, could meet important emotional goals for a sub-set of market consumers.

For relatively young, relatively affluent consumers, living in homes where difficult cleaning problems were the exception rather than the rule, the dominant emotional goal driver of detergent choice was no longer 'Will it clean?' but rather 'What does it say about me?' For these consumers, choosing Method products (which, by the way, clean perfectly adequately) and having their friends and family notice that they had chosen them – made a very positive statement about their lifestyle. It says: 'I'm cooler than the average person'; 'I'm funkier than the average person'; 'I'm greener than the average person' – and, in homes where cleaning was relatively easy and lifestyle was a priority, these statements drove more important emotional goals.

The results show the impact of this proposition. Method was founded in 2001 by two college friends Eric Ryan, a designer and marketer and Adam Lowry a chemical engineer. Just five years later, in 2006, Method was named the seventh-fastest-growing private company in the US. Today, it is a major player in the US cleaning products market and is sold in markets across the world.

To add a brief personal anecdote to illustrate the emotional power of the Method proposition: when I first discovered Method and brought some bottles home, my wife, Ruth, was obviously impressed. She loved the cool and unusual pack designs, the vibrant product colours and the funky, indulgent perfumes. She also convinced herself that she preferred to be buying a 'green' product!

Some days after bringing Method home for the first time I opened a kitchen cupboard to find it packed full of Method products – far more than we would ever have used. 'What are you doing?' I asked Ruth 'We've got about five years' worth of product here!' 'Oh, they're not for us' she replied 'I've bought them as gifts for my mum, my sister, your sister, your mum . . .'

Imagine a household cleaning product being so desirable that it could be given as a gift to others! That's the power of a product proposition that achieves genuine emotional connection. That's what Method has delivered.

The Method story shows clearly how putting Catnip Proposition principles to work *always* delivers strong growth results. Those principles are, of course: clear focus on a defined group of consumers (or consumer mind-sets) whose emotional needs are not yet 'owned' by another brand; identification of the key MoMI for these consumers; development of a compelling proposition that delivers against the emotions behind these moments better than competitors. Result: autopilot preference secured amongst those target customers, and growth reliably delivered.

Now – an important refinement of this thinking. While in many cases the essential elements of the Catnip Proposition all need to be present, there are a significant minority of cases where a specific performance edge is not necessary to deliver autopilot status. These are cases where the emotional goal drivers are met by delivering standard category performance alongside ownership of the key Moment of Maximum Emotional Impact. Let me provide a couple of examples to illustrate this:

Lynx

Lynx, the deodorant/body spray range positioned as an 'aid to seduction' for young men in their mid/late teens does not deliver any differentiating functional benefit. Its dryness and deodorant qualities, its fragrances and its packaging are not significantly better than other category competitors. But, unique in its category, Lynx's positioning has grabbed ownership of the 'seduction' emotional goal territory and this emotional differentiator is enough to deliver autopilot status amongst its target group.

Lynx does, of course, tick all the other essential Catnip Proposition boxes:

- *Clear focus against defined target customers*: Tick.
  Young men mid to late teens.
- *Identification of powerful MoMIs*: Big Tick.
  Moment of meeting attractive girls – and brilliantly powerful and consistent connection with this moment.
- *Development and delivery of proposition* to deliver against the drivers of that MoMI: Half a Tick.

Product, packaging, fragrance etc all functional, but not truly differentiating. In this case 'owning' the emotional connection with the category MoMI is enough to secure preference.

- *Marketing that dramatises the Proposition at the key MoMIs*: Big Tick. Hugely distinctive and powerful marketing campaign dramatising the moment that drives 'auto-pilot' choice for this consumer group.

Other brands in the sector positioned on more functional characteristics (like Sure on dryness or Dove on kindness to skin) need to provide a meaningful functional benefit alongside the emotional territory they are seeking to occupy. But Lynx is an example of a brand that has been able to attain autopilot status without a significant functional differentiator.

This phenomenon is also quite common in a category like alcoholic drinks where image plays much more strongly than functional attributes like appearance or taste. Brands like Fosters, Stella, Heineken all have different tastes – but none could claim to be 'better' than the others. Rather, their differentiation is achieved through the degree to which they are able to claim ownership of the emotions behind the category MoMIs at any point in time. Elsewhere in the category brands like Guinness, many 'bitters' and almost all craft beers do use functional attributes like appearance and taste to differentiate – illustrating that different goal territories require different combinations of attributes to secure autopilot status.

There is no hard-and-fast rule as to which products/categories require a clear functional differentiator and which do not. This can only be understood by drilling down into the emotional goal territories in each category and understanding what it takes to deliver against the dominant goals better than any competitors.

This brings me on to an essential caveat which must be understood when developing Catnip Propositions for any business. This is that the requirements of a Catnip Proposition in any given category are likely to evolve and change over time – sometimes quite suddenly. These changes might be driven by new technology, by the entry of new competitors, or by attitudinal changes in society. But many businesses have come unstuck by assuming that their once-successful propositions would remain so forever, thus failing to notice game-changing developments which rendered once-dominant propositions ineffective.

Changes in technology are perhaps the most obvious and are the most likely to be noticed by incumbent brands – but that does not make them any easier to respond to. Technology changes can, overnight, alter consumer expectations of the category – long-accepted levels of performance may no longer be adequate; characteristics that previously had no importance in the category can sometimes become essential; goals that had not been relevant can suddenly become dominant.

Perhaps the most obvious example of this is the breakthrough development in the mobile phone markets personified by the Apple iPhone.

The iPhone was not the first smartphone, but it certainly became the most successful. Famously, smartphone technology 'changed the game' in the mobile phone market from how efficient your call plan was, how ubiquitous your network reach was, how long your battery lasted, or how small and neat your hand-set was to a market that suddenly competed on apps, games and instant internet access. Consumer expectations changed overnight and suddenly the brands that had been dominant in the 'old world' could not meet the demands of the emotional goals suddenly facilitated by the smartphone revolution.

Other markets have seen similar technology-driven upheavals. The Dyson vacuum cleaner with its rolling ball and consequently superior manoeuvreability set new performance expectations for its category – and simultaneously introduced new standards of design excellence that made choice of vacuum cleaner something of a lifestyle statement.

Significant changes can also be driven by breakthrough developments in design or positioning, and these can be just as powerful as technology-driven innovations.

To reference the mighty Apple again, their original breakthrough product, the Apple Mac, revolutionised the way we thought about personal computers, not by introducing any amazing new functionality but by launching beautifully designed, highly colourful computers into a market that had previously been dominated by almost identical black (or white) boxes (with lots of clever stuff inside them).

Overnight, personal computer one-upmanship had gone from 'mine's got more gigabytes of computational power than yours' to 'mine looks cool – yours doesn't'!

This simple change enabled the category to access new combinations of emotional goals when choosing a computer – our choice could now incorporate goals like excitement, adventure and autonomy as well as the more functional efficiency-driven goals – and for increasing numbers of consumers these emotional goals quickly became dominant.

Responding to this as an established player with warehouses full of black boxes was incredibly difficult – hence Apple's huge, rapid success.

The Method case study referenced above is another example of how significant aesthetics changes can 'change the game' in a previously functionally driven category and bring into play a new set of emotional goals that suddenly become dominant for certain groups of consumers. Again, very hard to respond to if you are one of the brands that has been used to a category fighting a 'functional' battle for the past 50 years.

The third area of change is the most difficult for incumbent brands to notice and therefore to respond to. This is when society evolves and attitudes to a category, a brand, or a way of doing business suddenly 'tip' from one position to another.

An obvious recent example is the banking industry which, having been expected (and trusted) merely to look after our money reasonably effectively for hundreds of years, saw consumer attitudes changing markedly in the post-2008 financial crash period.

Because of the common perception that banks were at least in part responsible for the financial crash, consumers suddenly wanted to do business with brands that were not only financially efficient but also met new (and hard to define) ethical standards. While all the established banking brands are now working incredibly hard to demonstrate their commitment to their communities and to society's overall wellbeing, their position in these newly important areas is inherently weak; they risk being outflanked by the new generation of 'challenger banks' who have none of the old ethical baggage and so can appeal to emotional goals that traditional banks struggle with.

Responding to changes like these is very difficult for incumbent businesses for all the obvious reasons. But it can be done. The key is to notice emerging changes before they invalidate your proposition. Most businesses struggle to do this and so are forced to evolve their proposition not from a position of strength but under the pressure of declining sales and profit trends. The demise of once-mighty brands like Nokia in mobile phones, Dell in laptop computers, Wimpy burger restaurants, or early digital successes like Friends Reunited, all show how difficult it can be to notice significant changes and recognise when evolution of your proposition is needed. The recent, and ongoing, struggles of the once-dominant supermarket chains like Tesco and Asda in the face of the enhanced 'hard discounter' propositions of Aldi and Lidl are a very current example of businesses that should have picked up the importance of a changing competitive environment and adapted earlier.

Even when change happens late, it can still be effective if the brand concerned is strong enough, and if its management is ready to embrace significant changes to re-invent its Catnip Proposition as needed.

One excellent example of a brand managing to re-position itself in the face of significant attitudinal shifts against it is the way McDonalds responded in the mid- to late-2000s to a torrent of negative publicity and an increasingly hostile public. Check out the box below to see how McDonalds managed to 're-invent' and reposition itself to respond to these changes and re-establish growth.

Case Study: McDonalds repositions itself to regain 'Permission to Sell'

Back in the early 2000s McDonald's was in trouble. Having dominated fast food in global markets around the world since the early 1980s, consumers had fallen out of love with the company.

Its food was seen as predictable and dated. Its employment practices and ethical standards were under constant media attack (remember the vitriolic attacks on 'McJobs'?) and, worst of all, it was being called out as a major contributor to the global obesity epidemic – in particular the rising incidence of childhood obesity across the world. From the US, across Europe and into Asia McDonald's was under fierce attack for ruining the health of the world's kids – luring them in with its Happy Meals and free toy giveaways and then turning them into mini addicts craving its high-salt/high-sugar/high carb foods.

This anti-McDonald's sentiment probably peaked with the launch in 2004 of the film 'Supersize Me' produced by the American filmmaker Morgan Spurlock.

The film stars Spurlock and documents a month in which he ate nothing but McDonald's food. The film describes the impact of this unusual diet on his physical and psychological well-being, as well as exploring the influence of the fast-food industry in general, and McDonald's in particular, on contemporary lifestyles and dietary norms. Unsurprisingly, the film's findings did not make attractive reading for the McDonald's business – during his month on their food Spurlock gained 11.1 kg, increased his cholesterol levels significantly and experienced mood swings, sexual dysfunction and a general deterioration in both his physical and emotional health.

Unsurprisingly, the media took the opportunity this highly dramatic story provided to portray McDonald's as representing everything that is bad about modern consumerist society. Press articles about the malign effects of McDonald's food abounded; consumer groups pushed for legislative changes to force the company to change key aspects of its operation; sales fell in the US and elsewhere as the impact of the negative publicity spread around the globe.

Crucially, the torrent of negative publicity meant that McDonald's had lost the essential element of any relationship between a brand and its customers – the emotional connection that gives it 'permission to sell'. It wasn't that its food had become less tasty, that its restaurants had deteriorated or that its value had suddenly got much worse. All these things were the same. What had changed, though, was that the public's view of McDonald's had changed – the brand had gone from a friendly provider of fun family outings to a corporate predator exploiting their children's health to make profit. *Crucially, for many consumers, that emotional 'permission to sell' had been withdrawn.*

Once a brand loses this emotional connection, it is very hard to regain it. Perhaps the most difficult type of situation for a business to deal with is one where the change in consumer attitude has little to do with either the brand itself, or with its competitors – the change is due to societal attitudes altering. This was the situation McDonald's faced. Despite the magnitude of this challenge, McDonald's did indeed manage to rebuild its connection with its customers and re-establish that crucial 'permission to sell' which has enabled the growth it has enjoyed in recent years. How did the company achieve this turnaround?

Fundamentally, through McDonald's recognising that the basis for its traditional emotional connection with its customers – providing filling, great tasting, good value food – was no longer enough. Society's views had been changed by the torrent of negative publicity and the connection had, for many consumers, been broken. To restore it McDonald's had to change. And it did change.

In a rare case of corporate humility, the company recognised that it had to move away from some of the core elements of its traditional operating model. Within months of Morgan Spurlock's film being released McDonald's removed the 'Supersize' option from its menus.

Acknowledging that the public was no longer going to accept a menu dominated by burgers, fries and high-sugar drinks, McDonald's accelerated the development and introduction of much healthier, low-fat, low-carb, low-salt menu options including ranges of salads – products that would have been anathema to the 'old' McDonalds business.

Realising that its bright, low-cost, functional-but-basic restaurants had been overtaken by the much more comfortable surroundings provided by Starbucks and other coffee chains, McDonald's invested in a huge refurbishment programme in its restaurant chains. They became stylish, comfortable, inviting, they provided services like free Wifi access (one of the first chains to do this) and they sent a strong message of welcome and a new respectfulness to its customer base:

In an acknowledgement that they had to work incredibly hard to convince customers and opinion leaders that it was running its operation in a new, open and ethical way, it began to provide all sorts of previously unseen information about the nutritional content of its food, its environmental and other policies, and its approach to the employment and development of its staff. Booklets/leaflets describing 'The facts behind the flavours', 'The A-Z of our products . . . and what's inside them', 'Our environment' were made available in its restaurants and online and it actively welcomed interaction on these matters from its customers and the media.

In effect, McDonalds reinvented itself, from a traditional burgers 'n fries fast-food joint to a modern, stylish family restaurant – and in so doing, re-established the 'permission to sell' that its consumers had temporarily denied it during the immediate post-'Supersize Me' period.

With this permission re-established, McDonalds could once again drive its core proposition of great tasting, great-value food – and return to significant, sustained, profitable growth.

Not only that, but today McDonald's is regularly voted amongst the 'most loved' brands in the world – a position that would have been inconceivable in the dark days following the 'Supersize Me' episode. Brands can recover from even the most difficult positions if they are prepared to acknowledge how their customers are changing – and change with them.

To re-stress: the key is to monitor target consumer attitudes to your Catnip Proposition regularly – understanding both how well you deliver against the dominant emotional goals, understanding changes in how your competitors are perceived, and seeking to spot, early, developing changes in underlying consumer attitudes and needs. This requires tracking studies that can connect with the subconscious, emotionally – driven decision-making processes – not just conventional measures like 'satisfaction', 'liking' etc which are poor indicators of emotional connection. Such tracking tools do exist – but few companies are using them. This needs to change.

So – this chapter has attempted to explain the essential elements of a Catnip Proposition – a proposition which, if delivered, will secure autopilot status in your category, and how these elements need to be connected to deliver significant, sustained, profitable growth.

The evidence is very strong that, when companies develop, and execute, propositions based upon these elements they invariably see significant success – at least until their market, their competitors or their consumers change in some important way – at which point they need to reassess.

While developing a Catnip Proposition should have important implications for every element of a company's business, it has particular relevance and potential impact on the way brands are positioned and marketed. We believe that the insights and consumer understanding revealed in this book pose fundamental challenges for much conventional marketing thinking.

We turn to these challenges in our next chapter.

The Growth Director's Summary

- A 'Catnip Proposition' is a commercial offering that is so irresistible to target consumers that, if delivered, will secure guaranteed autopilot status and thus will deliver significant, sustained, profitable Good Growth for your brand.
- Delivery of your Catnip Proposition must drive all commercial activity across your business. All employees should be familiar with your Catnip Proposition and should be focused on delivering it.
- The key elements of a Catnip Proposition are:
  - it makes very clear which consumers (or consumer mind-sets) it is targeting – and is happy to de-prioritise others;
  - it is explicit about the MoMIs that it is seeking to connect with, and the emotions that lie behind them; and
  - it is clear about the differentiated performance promise it is making and is confident that this both sets it apart from other brands and connects meaningfully with the identified MoMI.

- In some cases (Lynx is one example, an alcoholic drink like beer is another) simply owning the emotional goal driver of the MoMI can deliver autopilot preference.
- Propositional elements required to deliver a Catnip Proposition are likely to change over time. Typical drivers of change are: technological developments; aesthetic/positioning-related changes; changes in consumer/societal attitudes
- Continuous tracking is needed to ensure you react to changes before the impact of your Catnip Proposition is affected. Tracking emotional attitudes to your brand is at least as important as tracking functional attributes.

Chapter 9

Marketing to Open Minds – i) Segmentation and Targeting: The new marketing paradigm and how it blows old segmentation thinking out of the water

Here's a famous quote:

> *Half the money I spend on advertising is wasted; the trouble is I don't know which half"*
>
> Lord Leverhulme, 1851–1925, founder of Unilever

Here are some less famous ones:

> 80% of new product launches fail
>
> Inez Blackburn, University of Toronto, 2008

> I'm not really very sure whether we're getting an acceptable return on our marketing spending. I think we could do a lot better.
>
> Finance Directors everywhere, since the dawn of time (a few CEOs too)

OK, the last one was made up – but the others are genuine, and illustrate a worrying truth – much of the marketing monies that are spent by consumer-facing companies are delivering a lot less than intended. In many cases, a lot of the money spent is just plain wasted.

After all, the fundamental purpose for which marketing funds are made available by CEOs is to ensure that businesses grow. As we saw way back at the beginning of this book, most companies, even the biggest, most 'successful' ones around have a very poor track record in delivering the growth numbers that they set themselves. Here's an illustrative (and rather remarkable) quote that appeared in Chapter 1:

- Since 2,000, 90% (of the companies in our surveys) have failed to hit the growth projections in their annual reports.

Allen (2014)

As this book has made clear, this failure is due to much more than just the effectiveness of these companies' marketing plans. However, it still raises serious questions about their effectiveness – or lack of it. Given the analysis that this book has presented, these rather dire statistics should come as no surprise.

Back in Chapter 2, I described The Big Growth Mistake that almost all consumer-facing companies make and how this leads to wasteful, inefficient commercial plans – which of course includes marketing plans. Let's remind ourselves of this mistake.

Companies build commercial plans on the assumption that all category purchases are potentially up for grabs – they're not.

In fact, most of the time as we have seen throughout this book, we shop on autopilot from a small portfolio of favourite brands with which we form emotional attachments and from which we are very reluctant to switch.

Sharp (2010) puts this very powerfully:

For reasons of habit or convenience we buy the same few brands over and over again and simplify buying decisions by only noticing our few regular brands.

The inevitable (and, for the marketing community rather awful) consequence of this truth is that, most of the time the consumers at whom we are targeting our marketing activity are just not paying attention in any meaningful way. They might see our ad, and might even enjoy it as a piece of creative work – but unless they are ready to make an autopilot choice, and unless the ad connects with the relevant Moment of Maximum Emotional Impact (MoMI) when autopilot decisions are made, then they will disregard it when it comes to making purchasing decisions.

Similarly, consumers might respond in-store to a particularly attractive promotional offer or deep price cut – but, once the offer is over, they will return (without even thinking about it) to their default autopilot favourite.

Much of the marketing activity out there is either speaking to existing autopilot consumers who would have bought the brand anyway, or it is trying and failing to change the minds of consumers who have made autopilot decisions in favour of other brands and are just not listening to any competing 'sales pitches'. No wonder the success stats for much marketing activity are so unimpressive.

In many ways, it is not inaccurate to characterise the effectiveness problem that much marketing has as being caused by *'marketing to closed minds'*. Once autopilot decisions have been made, we are rarely ready to listen to the propositions offered by other brands – our subconscious minds (the part of our brain that makes 90–95% of the decisions, remember) are 'closed' to other brands. In fact, being good at ignoring the 'tsunami' of marketing messages out there is one of the ways our subconscious brains have learnt to cope with the complexities of our lives.

'Marketing to closed minds' is not just a snappy phrase – it really does describe the defining problem for most of the marketing world: how do you ensure that the maximum amount of your marketing messages are reaching open minds – consumers with the genuine potential to buy your brand at a point when they are ready to consider doing so – and how do you ensure you are as persuasive with those open minds as it is possible for you to be once you have reached them?

The Growth Director says:

'Marketing to Open Minds' is the essential new marketing paradigm for growth.

- Most marketing programmes fail to deliver the growth they were designed to achieve – that's just a sad fact.
- Because we are hardwired to stick to our autopilot choices, we actively reject attempts to sell to us by competing brands. This means that, much of the time, marketeers are 'marketing to closed minds'.
- Directing marketing messages to those moments when consumers are ready to make autopilot choices, and communicating in a way that

secures 'permission to sell' is called 'Marketing at Open Minds'. This
should be the goal of all marketing spending.
- The keys to Marketing at Open Minds are:

  - targeting the right consumers/mind-sets – those with whom you have
    the best chance of securing autopilot status. Messages to other
    consumers are likely to be a waste of effort.
  - developing messaging which connects emotionally and thus secures
    'permission to sell'. This means presenting your product in the
    context of relevant Insights.
  - directing your marketing messages at, or evoking, the Moments of
    Maximum Emotional Impact when autopilot decisions are made.

Marketing at Open Minds

What does the marketing community need to do differently to become
expert at 'Marketing to Open Minds'?

A lot of the thinking I will present in the rest of this chapter is quite
challenging to conventional marketing thinking and planning.
Remember that the scientific foundations upon which this is based
have only emerged over the last 10 years or so (ie, since Daniel
Kahneman's Nobel Prize Winning neuroscience work in 2002). Most
of the thinking that drives conventional theories of marketing and
strategic planning were developed many years before that, when our
understanding of how our brains work was much less developed. It
should not be a surprise that, as we come to better understand the
way our brains guide our decision making, this will have a significant
impact on the ways we go about building and executing commercial
plans for our businesses.

While the thinking in this book has important implications for almost
all areas of marketing planning and execution, there are particularly
significant challenges to conventional thinking in three areas:

(1) *Targeting the right customers* – why conventional segmentation models
just do not work, and how to address this.

(2) *Developing the right messaging* – maximising your influence at the Moments of Maximum Emotional Impact and how much conventional marketing communications fail to do this.

(3) *Directing your marketing plans* – how to best avoid the significant media wastage caused by directing marketing messages at consumers whose minds are 'closed'.

I'll take each of these areas in turn. The first, targeting the right customers will be covered during the rest of this chapter. Developing the right messaging and directing your marketing plans for maximum effect will be the subject of Chapter 10.

Targeting the right customers

There is a fundamental problem with much of the segmentation work that goes on in consumer companies across the world. The problem is this: most segmentation models are consumer-centric.

'Consumer-centric' segmentation models? Doesn't sound like too much of a problem. Well, it is.

The problem with segmenting by type of consumer (typically by age, socio-demographics, income, expressed preferences, other buying habits etc) is that all such models make an implicit assumption that a given consumer is a consistent, predictable beast. This is just wrong.

As we discovered in Chapter 5, our actions are driven not by who we are (our age, occupation, level of wealth, life-stage etc) but by the emotional goals we are seeking to meet in any given situation. These goals are constantly shifting according to our circumstances and, as they do, this means we move into and out of the 'target group' for a particular brand. Conventional segmentation models just do not account for this truth and so are often inefficient by design.

Recall the goal territories map that we looked at in Chapter 5:

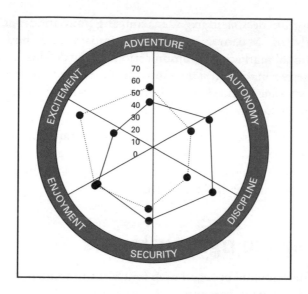

Figure 9.1

Source: Decode Goal Map reproduced with permission of Decode Marketing.

In any situation, a particular combination of emotional goals will drive our decisions, and as circumstances change so this combination will change too.

To illustrate, imagine the goal maps shown here represent the emotional goals of the same person choosing a holiday destination in two situations:

(a) Broken line: couple planning a holiday for themselves and prioritising excitement, adventure and enjoyment over security, discipline.
(b) Solid line: same couple planning family holiday with their children and now prioritising security and discipline over excitement, adventure.

Clearly, the holiday choices made by the same couple would be very different in the two situations described. A segmentation model which failed to take account of this would inevitably lead to significant wastage for either a company offering exotic, adventurous holidays for couples, or safe, enjoyable family-friendly vacations.

The simplistic holiday planning example given here provides a situation where the change in emotional goal priorities is obvious and easy to understand and to predict. However, the variability of the emotional goals driving our purchasing decisions holds true in all areas of our lives – and in all the brand choices we make.

Here's another easy-to-understand illustration. Take the three typical brands of beer available in almost every pub in the land:

- a 'blokey' lager, like Fosters
- a more sophisticated beer, like Stella Artois
- a traditional, local 'craft' beer, like Hopfest Pale Ale.

In different social situations a typical young male drinker might make very different choices between these three options. Out with his friends for the night he would probably choose Fosters, a brand which sends signals of male friendship and bonding and would satisfy emotional goals linked to enjoyment and security (security in the sense of strengthening bonds of friendship).

Out on a first date with a new girlfriend he might choose Stella Artois, a more sophisticated brand, enabling him to meet emotional goals tracing to excitement and autonomy ('I'm a more sophisticated guy than my Fosters-drinking mates – and I'm prepared to choose a less-masculine brand like Stella to signal my independence and autonomy').

In a bar with senior work colleagues perhaps he might choose the bottle of local craft beer to signal his maturity and sophistication ('You don't glug pints when you're out with the boss'). This enables him to meet emotional goals tracing to autonomy and discipline – attractive qualities to signal to important work colleagues.

The point here is that our decision making is driven not by who we are (socio-demographic criteria) but by the emotional goals driving us in any given situation (motivational criteria).

> The value we ascribe to products and brands is significantly influenced by the situational context we are in
>
> Barden (2013)

The key to effective segmentation is to target not consumers (whose emotional goal drivers and thus purchasing decisions will change according to their circumstances), but Emotional Goal Territories – the motivational goals that will drive purchase decisions and brand choices.

Importantly, since goals can often be satisfied by products from a range of different categories (a goal of providing a mid-morning snack might be fulfiled by a chocolate bar, a packet of crisps, some healthy nuts, a piece of fruit etc), segmenting markets by goal territories rather than consumer socio-demographics or product category definitions can often provide a brand with a bigger market opportunity than it had previously realised. So rather than being in the 'nuts' market, a brand may find it is actually in the much bigger 'snacks' market.

> Job-defined markets are generally much larger than product category-defined markets. Marketers who are stuck in the mental trap that equates market size with product categories don't understand whom they are competing against from the customer's point of view.
>
> Christensen, (2009).

A watch-out for consumer products companies is not to fall into simply defining your category according to the way your retailers range and display their products. Just because supermarkets choose to have a discrete area for 'nuts' does not mean that suppliers of nut products should define their market in this limited way.

Actually, in any market, a relatively small number of emotional goal 'footprints' will drive the vast majority of purchasing decisions, and it is these footprints that should form the basis of any segmentation model if it is to be effective.

Sometimes, emotional goal territories will cluster around a particular socio-demographic group, so it is useful to use socio-demographic criteria in targeting marketing activity. Lynx/Axe is an example of this. As we saw in Chapter 5, the map of Emotional Goal Territories for the deodorant/body spray market might look something like this:

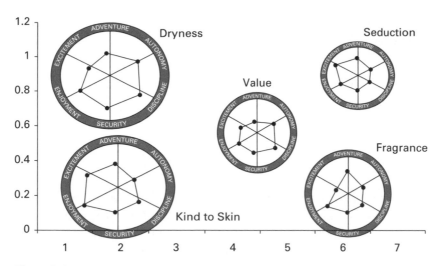

Figure 9.2

The Emotional Goal Territory driven by excitement/adventure and best described in this category as 'seduction' is populated almost exclusively by young males, and so it is easy, and sensible, for Lynx/Axe to use this simple socio-demographic marker in targeting its marketing activity. In most categories though, an approach driven by socio-demographic definitions of target customers is overly simplistic and is likely to be highly wasteful and largely inaccurate.

The 'choice of beer' example given above is one illustration of this – as would be that of the different ice-cream choices a consumer might make. Again, it is clear that in the different situations outlined below the choice of ice-cream by the same consumer (let's assume a 30-something mother with kids) is likely to be different:

• out with the kids: ice lollies/cones;
• out alone, moment of indulgence: 'exotic' brand – Magnum or similar;
• meal at home with the whole family: well known brand soft-scoop tub; or
• entertaining friends: 'sophisticated' brand/'interesting' flavours: Ben and Jerry's/Häagen Dazs.

A segmentation model in either of these situations that relied on socio-demographics as its basis would inevitably end up wasting significant amounts of marketing activity on consumers who, at the point they were exposed to its marketing messages, were not in a situation where they would be emotionally ready to respond.

Similarly, a segmentation model that implicitly assumes that its target 'occasions' or more accurately 'mind-sets' are confined to a particular socio-demographic is likely to miss the opportunity to secure purchase from many other types of consumer when they are driven by the combination of emotional goals that the brand in question would satisfy.

So – to take another obvious example, if desire for a Magnum is driven by emotional goals linked to personal indulgence (enjoyment/ adventure/autonomy) then effective targeting would seek to appeal to all consumers who enter this emotional goal territory on a reasonably frequent basis. While some types of consumer might be in this emotional territory more frequently than others (and so would be a higher-priority target group), a smart marketing plan would seek to own this territory (and the MoMIs when the emotions are most powerfully evoked) for all the diverse consumers who enter it from time to time. Clearly, this would not be confined to one or two socio-demographic categories.

A great example of a brand effectively targeting a powerful emotional goal territory rather than socio-demographics is the Dove 'Campaign for Real Beauty' that we looked at in Chapter 6.

Dove understood that the emotional drivers behind the campaign (the desire to feel comfortable and at ease with the way they looked) were relevant for almost all women at different times, so they constructed a campaign that explicitly reached out across traditional socio-demographics to appeal to older, younger, larger, slimmer, married, singles . . .

The breadth of the campaign's appeal seems obvious now – but it was actually highly unusual for beauty campaigns to pursue this type of broad appeal at that time. The conventional logic (driven, I wonder, by conventional segmentation studies?) was that beauty products for younger women must target them explicitly and exclude older women – and vice versa. Dove understood that it was not types of consumer it was targeting, but emotional motivations, and that, because these motivations existed for women across the socio-demographic range, it was therefore appropriate for the marketing campaign to utilise a similarly broad approach.

The challenge for marketing managers and media planners, of course, is that it is much easier to think about, and quantify, target segments in terms of simple socio-demographics. But this challenge must be taken on. Sharp (2010) writes about this with strong emphasis:

- No consumer is wedded to one attribute all the time. This is a common mistake made in segmentation research … Buyers use (for evaluation) different attributes at different points in time. Context can matter a lot.

The good news is that tools to enable this type of market mapping and segmentation do now exist. Post-Kahneman developments in neuroscience-based research/market mapping tools now enable businesses to map markets according to the Emotional Goal Territories that exist there and, crucially, to size these territories in terms of the proportion of category purchase occasions that each territory is responsible for driving.

Crucially, these tools are also capable of mapping the equities of the competing brands in a category onto that category's emotional goal territories so that any brand owner can understand territories where other brands have a much closer fit to the ideal than they do (so these territories should be avoided) and can identify the one or two territories where the emotional goal profile of their brand is as good as, or better than, all competing brands. This, of course, is the territory they should target – their Growth Sweet Spot.

To illustrate, had this exercise been completed on behalf of Lynx in the deodorant/body spray category, its equity fit compared to the emotional goal footprint driving category purchases might look something like this:

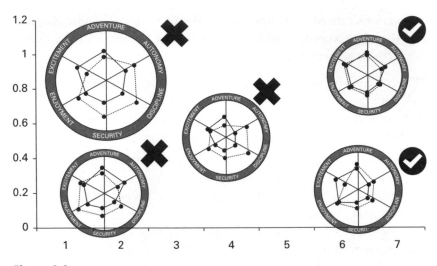

Figure 9.3

Broken line = emotional goal footprint driving purchase in the category
Solid line = Lynx equity footprint applied to each territory

As you should be able to see, the fit between Lynx's equity and the ideal emotional goal footprint is poor in the three categories with a big 'x' next to them. Further, there will be other brands whose equity fits much more closely with the ideal in these three territories (the likes of Sure, Dove etc). Attempting to build business in a territory where a competing brand has a better equity fit is very difficult, and should almost always be avoided. In the other two territories, however, the Lynx equity fit is good and, in the case of the top-right category (recall, this is the 'excitement/seduction' territory) the fit is almost perfect. Thus, a sensible brand would choose the best fit territory as its Growth Sweet Spot.

This is the only accurate way to derive a segmentation model which will efficiently direct commercial and marketing efforts at the highest-potential purchase occasions for your brand. To be successful, brands must target Emotional Goal Territories, NOT socio-demographic groups.

This is quite a challenging finding for traditional marketing planning and for many traditional marketing tools that make the implicit assumption that consumers are consistent, predictable beings and thus target marketing spending at pre-selected fixed socio-demographic definitions.

Perhaps the biggest challenge is for loyalty programmes, which have attracted huge amounts of marketing spending over the last 15 years or so. Loyalty programmes, by their very nature, work on the basis that consumers behave consistently and predictably and therefore seek to encourage increased loyalty by awarding points (which can later be redeemed for money) every time a purchase is made.

The analysis contained in this book would predict that loyalty programmes would have little impact on purchasing behaviour since their rewards are unrelated to the true reasons that consumers show loyalty or otherwise to a brand. Thus, this book's analysis would predict that loyalty programmes would merely heap extra rewards on consumers who had chosen a brand as their autopilot for reasons unrelated to loyalty rewards, and would have little affect in switching consumers who had other brands as their autopilot.

Independent research seems to indicate that this is exactly the behaviour that we see.

Byron Sharp and his team at the Bass Ehrenberg Institute spent much time analysing the impact of loyalty programmes for his book *How Brands Grow*. Their work was replicated on different brands by Professor Lars Meyer-Waarden and Christophe Benavent in France. From this additional research, Sharp concluded that loyalty programmes can affect loyalty, but the overall impact is very weak.

- Loyalty programmes are good at recruiting existing buyers of a brand ... but lousy at recruiting heavy category buyers who are not current buyers of a brand
- Loyalty programmes are not good at affecting loyalty

Both Sharp (2010)

This is, of course, a very serious conclusion for the many companies who spend millions of pounds each year on such programmes. Loyalty programmes are very expensive to run and are very hard to exit once they have been established. It does indeed look as if, in most cases, they have only a minimal positive impact on the growth performance of the brands who use them.

This is perhaps the single most obvious negative impact of failing to truly understand how consumers behave, and how to target the groups/

occasions/mind-sets with greatest potential – and perhaps underlines, more powerfully than any other single fact, why companies should be prepared to radically re-think their approach to customer targeting.

To re-state, once the target Emotional Goal Territory for a brand has been identified and quantified, it is then possible to 'drill down' into the territory to understand the characteristics of the consumers/consumer mind-sets that populate it. Sometimes – as in the case of Lynx/Axe – it will be found that the emotional goal footprint of the territory clusters around a particular socio-demographic group, and has little relevance outside of that group. In cases like this, of course, it then makes good sense to target commercial and marketing activity to this socio-demographic.

In many cases this will not be the case, and the emotional goal footprint will apply to a wide range of socio-demographic groups according to the circumstances they find themselves in. The only way to maximise a brand's appeal in these circumstances is to target the Emotional Goal Territory, not a particular socio-demographic.

So – to summarise the implications of the thinking presented in this book for segmentation and customer targeting:

- Purchase decisions and brand choice are driven not by who a consumer is, but by the emotional goals they are seeking to satisfy. These goals change according to circumstances.
- Because of this, segmentation and customer targeting driven by socio-demographics is often inaccurate and almost always inefficient and wasteful.
- The key to effective segmentation and customer targeting is to target by emotional goal territory – this is the only way to ensure efforts are directed at the consumers with whom you have greatest growth potential.
- Sometimes the highest potential emotional goal footprints will cluster around a particular socio-demographic group. In these cases using socio-demographic markers to target marketing activity can be highly effective (Lynx/Axe is a good example of this).
- More commonly, different types of consumer will move in and out of the emotional goal footprint at different times. The key in these cases is to target the emotional goal territories themselves,

not consumer socio-demographics. This will maximise your brand's appeal to ALL consumers with the potential to buy (Dove's Campaign for Real Beauty is an example of brand that has done this very well).

The Growth Director says:

Segmenting by emotional goals, not by socio-demographics is the key to effective targeting.

- Purchase decisions and brand choice are driven not by who a consumer is but by the emotional goals they are seeking to satisfy. These goals change according to circumstances.
- Because of this, segmentation and customer targeting driven by socio-demographics is often inaccurate and almost always inefficient and wasteful
- The key to effective segmentation is to target by emotional goal territory – this is the only way to ensure your efforts are directed at the consumers with whom you have the greatest growth potential
- Typically, consumers move in and out of different emotional goal territories as their circumstances change – target the emotional goal territory, not the consumer, and become autopilot for the circumstances where you can best 'win'.

But – hold on a minute. Doesn't this revelation that consumers move in and out of different emotional goal territories according to circumstances undermine the whole autopilot thinking that this book has made such a big deal about? After all, if consumers choose different brands according to their 'moods' then all that stuff about autopilots was bunkum.

Well – good point – but actually no. In fact this further explains and strengthens the autopilot thinking. Here's how:

Autopilot behaviour is linked to a set of emotional goal drivers rather than to an individual. To take the ice-cream example referred to earlier in this chapter, a consumer might have Magnum as an autopilot choice for a moment of personal indulgence, but a tub of Kelly's Cornish Dairy ice-cream for a family meal with the children.

Magnum is not interested in competing in the 'family ice-cream tub' market and Kelly's is not interested (and probably much less able) to compete for indulgent treats for individuals.

In effect, these are two separate markets (even though the core product is similar) and consumers will have their autopilot favourites for each of them. The question 'Which is your favourite ice-cream?' is not really a meaningful one: much more meaningful would be to ask 'What's your favourite for indulging yourself?' or 'What's your favourite for sharing with the kids?' etc

So – autopilot behaviour does, always, hold true – it is just that the category of purchase occasions for which an autopilot choice is maintained is driven by emotional goal drivers, not by functional definitions like 'ice-cream products'.

'Market-Making Customers'

There is one other very important implication of understanding that customer targeting and customer segmentation should be driven by emotional goal territories and not by socio-demographics. This is a phenomenon that I call the existence of crucial sub-groups of 'Market-Making Customers' who set the standards and influence the brand choices of all other consumers who enter the emotional goal territory.

At the heart of almost every emotional goal territory sits a group of consumers who are driven by that particular emotional goal 'footprint' every time they enter the category and who, by dint of their lives, are high-frequency category purchasers. These consumers are, first of all, a very important sub-group to understand and target because they account for a disproportionate share of all the purchases driven by the particular emotional goal footprint.

But, more importantly, it is likely that because they are frequent category purchasers and users, their behaviour, prejudices and choices will set the standards (or 'make the market') for all other brands to meet. By definition, because they are frequent purchasers, retailers and distributors will be highly sensitive to the brands they prefer and are likely to prioritise these in terms of listings, shelf space, promotional support etc. Further, because of their frequent usage – and therefore the relatively important place this category will have in their lives – these consumers will feel particularly strongly about the merits of the various brands in the market – and will be highly influential to other less frequent category purchasers.

So – regular business travellers using budget hotels (like me . . .) will probably have tried all the various different brands and will have decided which one they prefer. I always try to find a Premier Inn close to my business destination because of the passion they show towards ensuring their guests enjoy a good night's sleep and wake up refreshed and energised.

But – because my contacts and friends know I travel regularly they are likely to ask my advice when they are planning an overnight stay; because Premier Inn has become my personal autopilot choice, I will advocate this brand quite passionately, explaining why I am so impressed with what they offer (superior mattresses; choice of four pillow softnesses; a Good Night Guarantee etc) and actively try to persuade them to choose a Premier Inn. (For the record, I have absolutely no commercial relationship with Premier Inn – I just like what they do!)

My advocacy has two important beneficial effects for the Premier Inn brand: first, it undoubtedly gets them a lot of new user business that they would not otherwise have had; second, because their proposition is so clear, because I am very happy (indeed keen) to advocate it (and 'prove' to my friends how smart I am for choosing it) and because I am likely to be only one of many such advocates, the Premier Inn proposition (prioritising a good night's sleep over other types of offering) increasingly becomes seen as the market standard. Since they already 'own' this proposition and have an organisation focused on delivering it, they are in a very powerful competitive position.

Focusing on super-satisfying your Market Making Customers can give you all of these advantages.

This phenomenon has two implications for businesses. The first, obviously, is that, once the highest-potential emotional goal territory for your brand has been identified, you should work VERY hard to drill down into this territory and identify those high-frequency, high-passion Market Making Customers. This group is likely to be very willing to engage with companies wanting to understand their views on the market and the brands within it, and as you develop, refine and bring to market propositions and marketing programmes this is the group your research programmes should be targeting – relentlessly. Remember – if this group are super-satisfied with your brands then you can be very confident that all others entering the emotional goal territory will be similarly impressed – and that's how you become the autopilot choice for more and more consumers – and grow!

The second implication, though, is equally important – but much less obvious. This is that, if you can put suitable tracking programmes in place with the Market Making Customer group, they will be an incredibly effective 'canary in the coalmine' as the market evolves, competitors change, expectations and needs develop in new directions.

By dint of their frequency of purchase and passion for the category, your Market Making Customers are likely to be the first to spot/react to new trends/new brands/new ways of meeting their emotional goals. If you can keep close to this group then you have an incredibly effective way to spot developing trends/changes in attitudes to your brand/relative impact of competitor initiatives etc. This group use the category frequently – and they really care about it – so they will not only be the first to spot and react to any important category trends/changes but will articulate them with a clarity that you will find hard to get from less-frequent, less-engaged occasional user groups.

Most tracking studies are 'broad not deep'. They tend to survey all consumers in a particular market – and this often means that important trends get missed, or are at least not picked up until they are so meaningful that it is hard to respond to them.

A close focus on tracking behaviours, views and attitudes of the Market Making group is the best way to stay ahead of the curve in your market and spot the emergence of new trends before they become a threat to you.

So – step number 1 in building marketing plans that will drive significant, sustained, profitable growth: targeting the customers with whom you have the greatest chance of driving such growth through segmenting the market by emotional goal territories, NOT by socio-demographic factors.

This chapter has looked at how to do this, why it is so important, and how segmenting and targeting in this way not only ensures you minimise waste in your commercial and marketing plans and maximise your likelihood of growth, but also gives you access to a crucial core group of Market Making Customers who set the standards for the market, are highly influential with new/occasional users and who should form the basis for your research and tracking efforts.

We now need to move on to how, once your target consumers have been effectively identified you can (i) develop messaging that connects powerfully at the key moments when brand choice decisions are made and so secures default autopilot status for your brand and (ii) direct your media spending so that your message reaches your target consumers at the moments when they are listening – and ready to make an autopilot decision.

These subjects will be covered in Chapter 10.

The Growth Director's Summary

- Sadly, many marketing programmes fail to deliver the growth they are designed to achieve, resulting in the famous quote: *'Half of my marketing spending is wasted: I just don't know which half.'*
- As we are hardwired to stick to our autopilot brands, most of the time we are neither listening, nor receptive, to messages from competing brands. Much of the time we are 'Marketing to Closed Minds'.
- Directing marketing messages to those moments when consumers are ready to make autopilot choices, and communicating in a way that secures 'permission to sell' by connecting emotionally is called 'Marketing at Open Minds'. This should be the goal of all marketing spending.
- The key to 'Marketing at Open Minds' is:
    - targeting the right consumers/mindsets – those with whom you have the best chance of securing autopilot status;
    - developing the right messaging – connecting emotionally at the

  Moments of Maximum Emotional Impact to secure 'permission to sell'; and

 – directing your marketing plans at those key moments when autopilot decisions are made.

- The key to effective segmentation and customer targeting is to target by emotional goal territory – this is the only way to ensure efforts are directed at the consumers with whom you have greatest growth potential.
- Sometimes the highest potential emotional goal footprints will cluster around a particular socio-demographic group. In these cases using socio-demographic markers to target marketing activity can be highly effective (Lynx/Axe is a good example of this).
- More commonly different types of consumer will move in and out of the emotional goal footprint at different times – target the emotional goal territory NOT socio-demographic consumer types.
- Understand, and focus relentlessly on your Market Making Customers – those high-frequency, high-passion users who set the standards for the category and can be highly effective brand advocates.
- Track Market Making Customers over time for 'early warning' of changes to your brand's perception/threats to its 'autopilot' status.

Chapter 10

Marketing to Open Minds – ii) Bringing the Catnip Proposition to Life: The new marketing paradigm and how it blows old brand positioning thinking out of the water

Bringing the Catnip Proposition to life – and getting consumers to notice it

By now, we should have adequately established the importance of becoming completely clear about which consumers/consumer mindsets offer your business the best opportunity of becoming the default autopilot choice and therefore baking in significant, sustained, profitable growth for your brand and your business.

As the last chapter showed, getting your customer targeting right is absolutely fundamental to delivering Good Growth. The failure to understand which consumers/consumer mindsets offer the best chance of becoming the default autopilot and a consequent failure to focus commercial and marketing resources against this highest-potential group is a very common mistake, leads to huge wastage in marketing spending and makes growth most unlikely.

You MUST get your customer targeting right.

Chapter 9 examined traditional segmentation models, explained their shortcomings, and offered instead approaches to segmentation and customer targeting that are driven by emotional goal territories, not by socio-demographic criteria. Lets move forward on the assumption that this targeting has been completed effectively; given this assumption, we now need to examine the best ways of developing marketing messages that will secure autopilot status with your target customers, and consider how to direct your media and marketing spending so that it reaches your target consumers at the moments when they are listening and are ready to make an autopilot brand choice.

We should start by reminding ourselves of how rare it is to construct marketing plans that unequivocally deliver against their core purpose – generating growth. Go back to some of the stats and quotes I used earlier in the book to illustrate this dismal point: growth can be incredibly difficult to achieve.

Bringing the Catnip Proposition to life

The task of an effective marketing programme is simply to bring the Catnip Proposition to life for identified target customers at moments when they are ready to listen to it and to consider making an autopilot choice.

In essence, this defines the single critical element of a marketing director's job : if he/she fails in this task it is most unlikely that they will achieve the growth that is the objective of all marketing spending. If the Catnip Proposition is effectively communicated then growth will follow – for marketers, nothing is more important than this.

Remember from Chapter 6 how we explained that in order to persuade consumers of the power of your Catnip Proposition and secure their autopilot choice, your communication needs two essential elements:

(a) it must establish an emotional connection with your target consumers so as to secure their permission to sell; and
(b) it must present a differentiating performance promise that will be meaningfully preferred at the emotionally important moments when autopilot decisions are made.

To ensure that your target consumers notice your brand, engage with it at the key moments of autopilot choice and then actively choose it, your marketing plan must be super-effective at both these things. Let's consider each in turn.

Connecting emotionally to secure 'permission to sell'

Let's remind ourselves of why securing permission to sell is necessary in the first place. It's very important for all marketers to remember that our 'default setting' is NOT to be sold to. Partly as one element of the way we cope with the complexity of our lives (i.e. part of the way we try to reduce the impact of that complexity on us) and partly to strengthen our self-image as robust individuals who are 'not taken in by advertising and brands' we are pre-programmed both to ignore most of the advertising we are exposed to, and to reject most of the messages that do get though.

If marketers do not find ways to break through these barriers and render target consumers receptive to their messages, then these will either be ignored or rejected without proper consideration – in effect you will be *'marketing at closed minds'*. Let me re-stress for emphasis. Unless marketers find ways to open consumers up emotionally and thus gain permission to sell then even the most rationally persuasive messaging will be screened out or rejected. This is a crucial imperative which all marketers need to understand, focus against and address.

As Sharp (2010) comments:

> Buyers, in effect "decide" not to consider the vast majority of brands on the market. Instead, they notice a few, and quite often only one – this underpins their loyalty.

Others have noticed the same built-in tendency to ignore, or reject most of the marketing messages we receive. Genco et al (2013) state:

> Consumers may have built-in resistance to persuasive messages ... that can produce 'reverse priming' effects. Are your marketing messages speaking to your consumers' conscious minds but creating resistance in their nonconscious minds?

Very powerful, consistent, findings from those who have looked across the spectrum at how we react to advertising and marketing messages. And, of course, very worrying for most marketers. However, these views, well-researched and valid though they are, do not present the whole story. After all, we do react to many types of communication, from the marketing world and beyond. What makes those that we do respond to effective?

Well, it seems clear that to deal with the complexity of our lives and to 'protect' ourselves from opinions/approaches that would cause us to have to constantly re-examine our decisions we are hardwired to screen out communications that conflict with our pre-existing opinions; instead, we are positively orientated towards any communications or cues that signal an attitude to the world similar to our own, which serve to confirm the views (prejudices?) we already hold, or which show clear empathy with an opinion, or a set of feelings, which are particularly important to us.

A well-observed example of this phenomenon is what is known in politics as campaigning on 'dog whistle issues'. These are issues or opinions which, when expressed, will elicit immediate sympathy/ support from large groups of people whose prejudices/opinions/ values they seem to reflect and affirm. Politicians have become very good at spotting 'dog whistle issues' and using communication to build emotional connections between themselves and large groups of voters.

Examples of such issues which have had high impact with different voting groups in the UK over recent years have been immigration control; spending on the NHS; and attitudes to welfare claimants. For different voter groups, these issues have been sufficiently emotionally important that politicians who express views with which they have sympathy in these areas are likely to secure their support across the full spectrum of other political issues (the equivalent of an autopilot choice in the political world) and thus their vote.

The rise of UKIP in the UK has been one recent example of how 'dog whistle' messages on EU membership and immigration control have conferred significant voter support in local and indeed general elections.

For much of its history, UKIP's policies in areas other than these key 'dog whistle' areas were loosely formed and rarely articulated (the UKIP leader Nigel Farage famously declared his party's 2010 general election manifesto was 'drivel') but this did not matter to its voters. Rather, because UKIP showed such empathy with its target voters on the issues they cared most about – EU membership and control of immigration – those voters connected emotionally with them and remained resistant to the much more comprehensive and 'rational' pitches put to them by other political parties.

In the 2015 General Election in the UK, UKIP recorded an amazing 12.6% of the national vote.

Essentially, the way these messages work is by establishing an emotional connection between politician and voter group. The voter's subconscious reaction is: 'That politician thinks just like me. That probably means I'll like most of their other policies too. I'll vote for them.'

The skill for politicians lies in finding 'touchstone' issues which are so emotionally important to groups of voters that expressing empathetic views on these issues will open those voters up to listen to their views in other areas . . . and eventually to vote for them.

The skill of the most successful politicians of our times has not been on meticulously articulating the detail of their policy platforms, but rather by establishing emotional empathy with groups of voters, often via connecting on emotionally-important 'touchstone' issues.

Think of the electoral success of 'intuitive' politicians like Ronald Reagan, Bill Clinton, Barack Obama (at least in his pre-office 'Yes We Can' days) or, most recently (and memorably) Donald Trump compared to the much-less-successful logic-driven 'emotion-free' approaches of politicians like Al Gore, or Hillary Clinton. Similar parallels could be found in UK politics between the intuitive, emotional connection of the likes of Margaret Thatcher, Tony Blair, Boris Johnson compared to the highly rational but much less successful styles of Gordon Brown, Ed Miliband and others.

Emotional connection is NOT an option – without it you will simply not be heard. If brands do not succeed in connecting emotionally then they will not secure permission to sell – and will be attempting to sell to consumers whose minds are closed to their efforts. The most successful brands 'get' this.

In the same way that politicians need to find issues that are sufficiently emotionally important to voters that demonstrating empathy on these subjects will give them permission to sell their party to voters on other subjects (and eventually to claim their vote) so marketers need to identify, and connect with, the emotions behind the goal territories driving product purchase decisions, and the moments when these emotions are most intense. Showing target consumers that you understand the importance of these emotions (and those key MoMIs) and that you empathise with the way they are feeling about them will deliver an emotional connection with these consumers and secure for your brand that crucial permission to sell.

Without this emotional permission you are most unlikely to secure autopilot status no matter how persuasive you are about the superiority of your product's performance. Without this permission you are unlikely to get your target consumer's attention in the first place; even if this is secured, your 'pitch' is unlikely to be accepted – we like to do business with people/brands (and politicians) that we like/ empathise with – we reject those for whom we feel little emotional connection.

Marketers MUST lead the way in identifying these emotions and the moments when they are most intense and then in creating communications materials that evoke them effectively. This is probably the key communications task for marketers everywhere. We describe marketing which is successful in establishing this emotional connection as *Marketing at Open Minds*.

The Growth Director says:
Connecting emotionally is key – without this you will not sell!

- The single key task for all marketers is to bring his/her brand's Catnip Proposition to its target consumers impactfully and persuasively.
- Without an emotional connection with your target consumers you will be denied 'permission to sell' and may even generate 'an automatic and non-conscious counter-persuasion reaction' against your brand – our brains have hardwired us to be resistant to communications from brands that are not our current autopilot choice.
- The key to securing permission to sell is to show consumers you understand/empathise with their view of the category and its emotional goal drivers.
- To secure this empathetic connection, you need to present your product and its benefits in the context of the moments that are most emotionally important to your target consumers – MoMIs.

Let's look at some examples of brands who do this very well.

A stand-out example of a brand that has secured permission to sell from its target customers in a very direct and powerful way is a brand that I have returned to (without apologies!) a number of times in this book: the deodorant/body spray Lynx/Axe. Lynx's target customers are young men, and the emotional goal territory driving this group when considering purchases in the deodorant/body spray category is best summarised as being about 'seduction' – making themselves more attractive to young women.

Lynx's marketing plan has done a great (if slightly unsubtle!) job in showing its target customers that it understands and empathises with these emotional goals. By dint of the visuals used (relatively nerdy guys attracting ridiculously attractive girls), comically exaggerated advertising claims ('spray more – get more') and a brand tonality/advertising style designed to appeal to the humour and attitudes of the target group, Lynx has done a great job of connecting emotionally with these customers. With this connection established, and thus permission to sell secured, the brand has then been able to present its variants/fragrances/performance claims to a receptive target customer group. In effect it has been able to ensure it is consistently marketing at open minds – and has become the default autopilot choice for its target customers as a result, driving significant growth.

A second excellent example of the power of emotional connection securing permission to sell would be the Christmas advertisements run by the John Lewis department store in the UK over the past few years.

Prior to this series, retail marketing at Christmas had been characterised by advertisements which were effectively extended showcases for the best of each retailer's Christmas products. Expensively shot, beautifully produced and designed to elicit a response of 'wow ... I want that!' these ads were very strong indeed on rational 'sell'. Typically, they would show a range of best-selling products in attractive Christmas surroundings usually being enjoyed by happy customers. Particularly attractive product features would be highlighted. New or unique properties would be shown off. Often, special offers would be available to make the purchase even more irresistible.

Now, there's nothing wrong with advertisements that showcase your products. It's natural to want consumers to see the best of your Christmas product ranges and to make advertisements to do just that. But, despite all the money and expertise that went into these ads, none of them have been able to match the impact, or the sales performance delivered by a very different retail campaign – the John Lewis campaign.

Typically, the John Lewis advertisements feature just a single product – and this from a store with a range of over 10,000 products. Often, the featured product would not even be a big seller. And yet, these ads have become the most successful, the most admired and the most talked-about Christmas ads – to the extent that the launch of the John Lewis Christmas ad is now a consumer and media event in its own right. More importantly, these ads have driven significant above-market growth for John Lewis over the key Christmas trading period year after year.

This success has been achieved not by showcasing (or, 'selling' – to which we are, remember, instinctively resistant) the store's most attractive products, but rather by capturing the emotional heart of gift-giving at Christmas, appropriating this for the John Lewis brand and thus securing permission to sell from the shoppers of the UK.

Typically, the ads will tell a story of one person buying a particularly well-chosen product for another. Recent examples are – a cartoon hare buying a cartoon bear an alarm clock so he can awake from hibernation for Christmas; a snowman buying a gift for his snowgirlfriend before they both melt; a little boy buying a companion for his (imaginary friend) toy penguin; a little girl buying a telescope for the lonely old man who lives on the moon.

In each case the films evoke the true emotion behind gift-giving at Christmas – not, actually, the desire to have the best and most expensive gifts, but rather to choose gifts so thoughtfully that the recipient is genuinely moved by them – in the case of the Man on the Moon in the Christmas 2015 ad, moved to tears. Isn't this the emotional reaction we all hope to elicit when we give our Christmas gifts to loved ones?

By understanding and evoking this powerful emotion, John Lewis is able to connect incredibly powerfully with everyone buying gifts for loved ones (er . . . that's all of us) and open us up to the idea of shopping for Christmas gifts at their store. They have secured our permission to sell – and their series of record-breaking Christmas sales figures bear testimony to the impact this has had on their business.

These two examples illustrate powerfully how marketers can identify and then seek to evoke the emotions driving purchase decisions in your category. Both these campaigns have not only understood the emotional territory driving category purchasing with its target consumers (for Lynx – attracting girls; for John Lewis – giving great gifts at Christmas) but they have identified the moments when these emotions are at their most intense – for Lynx, the moment when a young man first meets an attractive new girl; for John Lewis, the moment a loved one receives, opens and reacts to your gift.

So – as marketers, your tasks in securing permission to sell for your brand are as follows.

(1) Understand the emotional goal territory driving purchases of your target customers in your chosen category.
(2) Identify the MoMI when the emotions involved are at their most intense and when autopilot decisions are made.
(3) Ensure your marketing and advertising campaigns evoke and connect with these emotions so that your target consumers will be emotionally open to you and ready to listen to the more rational aspects of your proposition.

As Chapter 9 explained, the easiest way to do this is to identify the high-frequency Market Making Customers who will sit at the heart of your chosen goal territory and 'go to school' on their usage, attitudes and emotions. 'Going to school' on these customers means, at minimum, ensuring you understand when and why they use your products or services, when the performance of these are most important to them and why, what alternatives to your brand they consider using and when/why they choose you or a competitor, and what they believe the relative strengths and weaknesses of your brand is versus its competitors.

This understanding can be built up to some extent through conventional research – studying usage and habits data, through panel studies of purchasing behaviour, through focus groups and 'depth interviews' with individual customers, through spending time in home or in store with these customers, observing their behaviour and discussing this with them.

I also strongly recommend, though, the use of neuroscience-based/'implicit' research tools to understand the emotions driving the key decision-making moments. Such tools are increasingly available and, unlike conventional focus groups/customer surveys/consumer panels etc can connect effectively with our subconscious decision-making processes and the emotions which drive them. Conventional research just cannot provide this level of insight into our subconscious decision-making – its interaction is with our conscious brains only. You might 'get lucky' with conventional research and unearth a genuine emotional insight – but your chances are significantly enhanced if you can utilise neuroscience-based tools.

Ultimately though, and however you do it, remember that without this permission to sell your marketing messages are unlikely to be effective – we are hardwired to resist 'selling' messages. Finding a way to break this resistance down is essential to the success of your marketing plans.

At the end of this chapter you'll find an interesting Boots case study describing how securing 'permission to sell' was crucial in turning around its ailing Beauty business, and how this was achieved.

So – lets assume that you have identified the emotions behind the MoMIs in your chosen category and that your marketing plans are set up to connect with these. This brings us on to the second part of the challenge of bringing your Catnip Proposition to life – presenting a differentiating performance promise.

Presenting a differentiating performance promise

For most marketers, this element of the Catnip Proposition is much easier. We like thinking of ourselves as rational beings, and the business world teaches us to make decisions in an overwhelmingly rational way. Most companies see the core purpose of their marketing programmes as explaining, rationally, why their products are better than those of their competitors.

And there's nothing wrong with that. As long, that is, as we remember two things :

(a) without the emotional connection to secure permission to sell as outlined above your rational messages will either not be listened to, or will be screened out; and

(b) the performance elements that count are those that matter at the key MoMIs when autopilot decisions are made – you MUST focus on these, and be prepared to de-prioritise (or better still, ignore) other performance elements.

Let's examine the second of these points: communicating meaningfully differentiated performance at the moments when consumers care about it most – and when autopilot decisions are made.

Our brains do not see performance as being equal in all situations – rather our subconscious brains are acutely sensitive to the situations where performance is most important to us – for our subconscious brains, context is everything. Recall the analysis presented in Chapter 7 on this subject showing how our subconscious brains will remember the situations where product performance is most important to us and will choose the brands judged most likely to perform best in those situations.

Many of the companies who are most successful at securing autopilot status in their markets have similarly understood the situations where performance has highest emotional significance, and have skewed their propositions, and their marketing communications programmes to focus relentlessly on these.

Returning again to one of my oft-quoted examples: Premier Inn. This brand has understood that for its customers, seeking budget accommodation for one or two nights, the MoMI is when a customer wakes in the morning refreshed, re-energised and ready for a great day. Premier Inn has stripped the cost from non-essential areas of their operation (no mini-bars; no fluffy dressing gowns; no gyms etc) to invest in performance elements that enable them to out-perform all competitors at these key moments: highest-quality mattresses; four choices of pillow softness; the 'Good Night Sleep Guarantee' etc and so have developed a proposition which secures autopilot preference with their target customers because it delivers clear superiority at the moments when this matters most.

Similarly, their marketing programmes emphasise only those performance elements which support this Catnip Proposition: their brand campaign idea is 'Wake Up Wonderful' (tick!); their ads feature a well-known celebrity waking up refreshed and energised in a variety of situations (tick!); their web-site prominently features the Good Night Guarantee (tick!); at every check-in experience Premier Inn staff explain this guarantee and their commitment to it (tick!). Result – autopilot status secured and significant, profitable growth delivered year after year.

Another similarly impressive example of a brand focusing on superior performance at the key MoMI would be Asda in the days it was running its 'pocket tap' campaign, which focused on how leaving the check-out at the end of a family shopping excursion feeling that you had more money left in your pocket than you expected. This delivered both rationally and emotionally against the key driver of autopilot choice for middle- to low-income families deciding where to do their grocery shopping.

This campaign focuses on the key 'moment of truth' for shopping value – paying your bill at the checkout (tick); it explains the key differentiating benefit that Asda offers – lower prices on everyday groceries (tick); and it connects emotionally by showing the satisfied 'pocket tap' of a mum who has got great value for her family (big tick).

This campaign, which has been used a number of times over the years by Asda, is consistently associated with their strongest periods of growth.

So – we have looked at how to develop marketing programmes which *both* connect emotionally with target customers to secure permission to sell *and* present a differentiating performance promise which delivers superior outcomes at the key moments when autopilot decisions are made – in essence which bring a Catnip Proposition to life.

That brings us onto the final subject which this chapter will cover – how to target your marketing messages so that they are noticed, listened to and thus secure autopilot status – and growth – for your business.

The first point to re-stress is that to deliver significant, sustained, profitable growth (Good Growth) your marketing focus MUST be on growth through increasing penetration (i.e. by recruiting more customers week after week, year after year) NOT on trying to increase sales from your current users. This can only be delivered (profitably) when you have developed a Catnip Proposition that has the power to attract increasing numbers of your target customers because it meets their needs at the key MoMIs better than all competitors.

Many businesses make the mistake of overly focusing on their current consumer base in their marketing efforts. This often seems an attractive, and cost effective, approach: after all, these customers already buy us, therefore they already 'like' us, therefore it must be easier to get incremental sales from this group than from all the intransigent others who have rejected us so far.

Sharp (2010) presents large amounts of analysis to show how this focus on existing users is a big mistake, and how sustained, significant growth can only be delivered by constantly attracting new users. I will not attempt to reproduce his comprehensive analysis here (although I strongly recommend that you read his book) but will confine myself to quoting a couple of the key conclusions that he (and others who have worked in the same area) have reached:

> Brands grow primarily by increasing their market penetration.
> Sharp (2010) quoting work from Anschuetz 2002;
> Baldinger, Blair and Echambadi 2002; Stern and
> Ehrenberg 2003

> Growth is due to extraordinary (customer) acquisition. Contraction is due to dismal acquisition.
> Sharp (2010)

This last observation was confirmed by an extensive 2003 study by Erica Riebe working in the US and France on a range of brands and categories including shampoo, chocolate, pharmaceuticals and banking. The evidence is clear – to grow you MUST focus on attracting new users.

The one crucial piece of analysis that this book would add to Sharp's work are the insights that (i) purchase decisions are not driven by the socio-demographic profile of a consumer, but rather by the emotional goal territory that they are in; and (ii) consumers are likely to move in and out of a particular emotional goal territory according to their circumstances/situational context/mood etc.

So – assuming that your current users are automatically going to be your best sources of business in the next period of time is to misunderstand how purchase decisions are taken. Some of your current users will still be in the appropriate emotional goal territory and therefore will be a prime source of business for you – but many will not; directing your marketing efforts at them will be largely wasted.

Crucially, the task for your marketing programme is not to target a particular group of consumers, but rather to target an emotional goal territory and to secure the largest possible share of the purchases driven by this goal footprint. This is a fundamentally different approach to that taken by most companies/media planners – understanding its implications for marketing planning and execution is essential for all marketers in all business sectors. This presents some obvious challenges to traditional marketing planning thinking. After all, targeting a particular socio-demographic group is relatively easy – I can find out where this group live, what their interests are, which television programmes they watch, which their favourite online sites are etc. How do I go about targeting something as ephemeral as an 'emotional goal territory'?

The key, of course, is in the analysis presented earlier in this book of how our subconscious brains guide us to take purchasing decisions. You will recall that these decisions are driven largely by emotional factors and that purchase decisions, brand preference and, crucially, autopilot choice are driven by choosing the brand that best satisfies the anticipated needs of the key MoMIs – when the performance of the product or service in question has the biggest emotional impact on us.

So – the challenge for marketing/media planners is to target messages either at the MoMIs themselves, or at times when consumers are open to thinking about them – I call these Moments of Maximum Propensity (MoMAPs). The correct balance between targeting MoMIs and MoMAPs varies according to each category. Let's look at some examples.

In some categories, consumers are really only open to considering autopilot choices when they are experiencing the Moments of Maximum Emotional Impact.

One obvious example of this is seasonal gifts – or indeed seasonal food. It is obviously extremely unproductive to market Christmas gifts in mid-summer: no matter how well the moment of gift-giving is evoked, consumers are just not ready to consider Christmas gift options at this time of year and, in the summer months when their emotional energy is directed to summer holidays, would be most unlikely to engage emotionally with any company who tried to 'pitch' Christmas gifts to them. Permission to sell would be denied!

Another, perhaps less obvious, example is in financial services. During my time as Chief Marketing Officer at Barclays Retail/Business Bank, research showed that, of all the many interactions a typical consumer had with their bank over their lifetime, there were a small number of crucial, emotionally-important interactions that drove preference for one brand over another (banking MoMIs).

These were the few occasions when the outcome of the interaction had high emotional importance to a consumer: applying for a loan (real fear of embarrassment/sense of failure if turned down); applying for a mortgage (gateway to purchasing a new home); making pension investment decisions (securing your future). At these moments, the emotional engagement of the consumer was shown to be very high, and the bank's behaviour – in particular its empathy with the consumers' emotional needs – could switch autopilot choice from one bank to another.

Interaction at all other times was much less emotionally important and, no matter how good or how bad these experiences were, they would be most unlikely to shift autopilot preference. The challenge for the bank, therefore, was to develop products/services that would outperform all competitors at this small number of crucial, emotionally important moments, and then target marketing communications to consumers who were entering/in one of these moments. Pitching a wonderful new mortgage product to consumers who are not thinking about buying a home is wasted effort. Ditto loans, pension products etc. Once that same consumer reaches a lifestage or experiences circumstances where they are entering one of these moments, however, they will suddenly become super-receptive to the right marketing messages, and are potentially available to make an autopilot choice.

So, in these cases – Christmas gifting, banking services – the marketing challenge is to engage with consumers who are in/about to enter the Moment of Maximum Emotional Impact. For Christmas gifting this is relatively easy (we all know when Christmas is!) and mass marketing techniques like TV/outdoor advertising at the appropriate time of year will do the job. Banking requires a much more thoughtful approach, utilising extensive customer data/CRM techniques to identify and target lifestage/personal circumstance changes that might indicate a relevant moment is being reached.

The point is, in some categories marketers must target the MoMIs themselves – communication at other times just will not be effective. But this is not the case in all categories.

In many cases, particularly categories where we have more frequent experience of the key moments, consumers are able to 'imagine' the emotions they will experience when they reach the MoMI itself, so the MoMI can be evoked and autopilot choices can be secured. This 'marketing by evoking moments' tends to be most effective when three conditions hold true:

(1) A consumer is close enough to a MoMI that its consideration feels relevant.
(2) A consumer is able to engage emotionally with the anticipation of the MoMI even if it has not yet arrived.
(3) The consumer has time to consider alternatives to their usual autopilot – without this, they will invariably default to the existing favourite.

Let's consider some examples of where 'marketing by evoking MoMIs' is particularly effective.

An interesting example of this approach is in the market for summer holidays. Typically, marketing for summer holidays begins during the break between Christmas and New Year – some six months before the holiday will usually be taken. Despite this time gap, it appears clear that we are able to engage emotionally with the thought of flying somewhere exotic to lie on a beach even while we are in the depths of our winter. Interestingly, this contrasts powerfully with our unwillingness to engage emotionally with Christmas messaging during the summer months.

Nevertheless, the travel industry has learned that the emotional goals that drive holiday choice can be effectively evoked during the Christmas holidays – with the additional bonus that consumers typically have time on their hands in which to consider alternatives, and are often surrounded by the people that they will go on holiday with – family and friends. Result – a highly effective opportunity for marketers to evoke the decision-making moments and secure autopilot choice.

Marketing by evoking MoMIs is also highly effective in product categories where purchase frequency is high –therefore it is easy for us to engage with the emotions connected with the Moments of Maximum Emotional Impact even if we are not in such a moment when we view the advertising. My frequently-used examples of Lynx/Axe deodorant/body spray and Premier Inn hotels both illustrate this.

Lynx/Axe does not require its target young male consumers to be about to attend a party full of attractive girls – it just needs its targets to be able to imagine, and connect emotionally with such a situation occurring at some point in the (not too distant) future. For this target group this is not a difficult thing to imagine!

Similarly, Premier Inn does not need viewers of its advertising to be about to stay in budget hotels – but they do need them to be able to imagine such a situation and connect with the emotions linked to waking up refreshed and re-energised.

Taking a slightly less obvious example from a frequently purchased consumer product category: the wonderful 'Gorilla' advertisement for Cadbury's Dairy Milk Chocolate some years ago was able to evoke a moment of pure personal indulgence (in the case of the advertisement a gorilla anticipating, and then playing, a famous drum 'riff' with complete emotional abandon) and then link it to the (slightly less dramatic) moment of indulgence when we enjoy a slab of good, creamy, chocolate. Whether or not you were about to eat chocolate, the advertisement evoked the emotions of that moment of indulgence and appropriated them for the Cadbury's Dairy Milk brand.

So – whether by targeting the MoMIs directly, or whether by evoking them, the key to securing as big a share of the purchases in your chosen emotional goal territory as possible is to own these moments – and the key task for any marketing team is to create marketing and advertising plans that do just this.

In cases where the moments can only be connected with emotionally when consumers are about to experience them (such as the banking example given above) this requires targeted marketing techniques utilising data-driven CRM programmes, highly targeted digital media, social media campaigns etc. These have become increasingly commonplace over recent years – driving much of the compulsive interest in 'Big Data' (the ever-increasing quantities of data about their customers' lives and purchasing habits held by most consumer companies).

Interestingly, though, in many categories, the Moments of Maximum Emotional Impact can be highly effectively evoked as long as the consumer is ready to engage emotionally with the moment – they do not need to be actually 'in the moment' to engage emotionally with it.

The Growth Director says:
Catnip Propositions must be built around MoMIs – if you are to secure autopilot status nothing else matters

- Moments of Maximum Emotional Impact are where autopilot decisions are made.
- To secure autopilot status you must first connect with the emotions driving these MoMIs to secure 'permission to sell' from your target consumers.
- Once permission to sell is secured, you must present a differentiating performance promise that persuades consumers that your brand will deliver better than all others at the key MoMIs – this means delivering better than other brands on the performance elements that matter most at the MoMIs – this is when autopilot decisions are made.
- Marketing communications are most effective either

    - when delivered at the MoMI itself, or
    - when they effectively evoke the MoMI whenever they are encountered.

But – how does a marketer know this? How can he/she distinguish between two potential consumers, one of whom is ready to engage with a well-evoked moment, and the other who is not yet ready? The answer is NOT to attempt to crunch your 'Big Data' down further to identify emotional readiness for engagement by individual consumers – you will just not be able to do it.

The answer, rather unfashionably, is mass media – good old-fashioned TV, outdoor, print advertising etc. Really? Why?

In the age of Big Data, mass media has come to be seen as unsophisticated, imprecise and inefficient. And, if the game is targeting consumers according to socio-demographics or past purchasing behaviour then that is true. In a world driven by emotional goal drivers, however, where the marketing planning task is to engage with those consumers who are ready to connect emotionally, highly targeted campaigns driven by the uber-rationality of Big Data are of little use – and are likely to be highly ineffective, often connecting with consumers at a time when they are not ready to engage in this way.

Mass media, though, while socio-demographically dumb, is emotionally highly smart. It enables a marketer to broadcast well-developed, emotionally engaging message that will highly effectively evoke the Moments of Maximum Emotional Impact. Smarter still, rather than attempting the impossible task of identifying and targeting consumers who are ready to engage emotionally, mass media works not only by attracting the attention of all those consumers in the target group who are already prepared to engage in this way, but, through skilfully evoking the Moment of Maximum Emotional Impact will move others from a 'non-engaged' to a 'ready to engage' emotional state.

In effect, mass media enables every one of the consumers who are potentially driven by the emotional goals behind your selected territory to 'opt in' to connecting with this messaging. Mass media effectively allows 'self selection' by 100% of the potentially engaged consumers out there – a much higher level of impact than could be achieved by even the most sophisticated Big Data-driven targeting.

That's smart!

Obviously, the efficiency of any form of mass media can be significantly improved by intelligent media placement – Lynx/Axe should target TV programmes/publications/websites frequented by its young male target audience – but in most cases, mass media will outperform highly targeted media when the task is to evoke MoMIs across a large consumer group.

So – a very important challenge is raised to the increasing dominance of Big Data-driven, highly targeted marketing campaigns: if the task at hand is purely to identify and target socio-demographic groups with transactional messaging then this approach can work well; but if the challenge is to engage emotionally with consumers at the point when they are entering the emotional goal territory targeted by your business, then mass media is likely to be a much more cost-effective option.

While Big Data is extremely effective in telling you WHAT people do, Brain Data tells you WHY they do it – and therefore is much more effective at providing the understanding necessary to predict or affect future choices. Without the context and emotional insights that Brain Data provides, Big Data is at risk of being of little value or at worst misleading. And since most marketing spending is aiming at influencing future choices, this means that most of the time Brain Data beats Big Data!

In conclusion – over the last two chapters we've seen how new thinking about how the brain works, how we make purchasing decisions and brand choices and how we respond to advertising lays down some fairly fundamental challenges for traditional ways of planning and implementing marketing campaigns.

For marketers prepared to respond to this new thinking, however, the opportunities are substantial. The truth is that much of the thinking behind traditional marketing plans is somewhat flawed, and those companies and those marketers who embrace the enhanced understandings we now have of how our brains work can secure significant commercial advantage for their businesses and their brands.

This book has attempted to lay out clearly how to re-position brands to enable them to achieve significant, sustained, profitable Good Growth. It has covered how to target the customers with whom your brand has the greatest growth potential, how to connect emotionally with those customers to secure their permission to sell, how to develop and bring to market Catnip Propositions that will secure autopilot status for your brands and how to develop and implement marketing programmes that will be noticed, listened to and positively responded to by your target customers.

All seems enormously straightforward, doesn't it?

Well – to an extent, yes it is. Of course, since Real Life is never as simple and rational as the chapters of a book can imply, there are many risks and potential pitfalls that could cause even the most focused and brain-science-savvy company to fail to grow to its potential.

This brings me to my concluding chapter (at least, to the chapter before the Summary chapter ….) which attempts to answer the question 'So – what could possibly go wrong?'

Case Study: How Restoring 'Permission to Shop' Drove Growth for Boots' Beauty Business; *by Ian Filby, CEO DFS*

Ian Filby has been Chief Executive Officer of the DFS furniture chain since late 2010. However, earlier in his career, he was responsible for managing the crucial Beauty category at the Health and Beauty retailer, Boots.

Ian led the category into growth from a period where it had lost connection and 'permission to sell' with its core target customer group. This case study describes how 'permission to sell' was regained.

'When I took over running the Boots Beauty business it was not a very fashionable place for women to go for beauty products.

Boots' reputation had always been in healthcare, and this had driven its brand profile for many years – everyone had memories of being taken to Boots by their mother when they had a cold as a child.

All great as far as it went – but it gave us a bit of a problem on the Beauty business. Our task was to persuade women that Boots – that good old cough mixture and plasters retailer – was the place to go to when they wanted to enjoy an indulgent shop finding wonderful new products to make them look and feel gorgeous.

Key to the work we did was recognising that the shopping journey a customer was on when she chose to buy beauty products was emotionally very different to when she was shopping for toiletries or healthcare products. For these latter categories the trip was a much more functional one. It was about enabling her to find the products she wanted quickly, at good value, and to complete her shopping trip as efficiently as possible.

Beauty is different. Even if a shopper combines a beauty shop with toiletries or healthcare products, her emotional state is different when she is in beauty buying mode. We had to create an environment where she would feel comfortable engaging in this type of indulgent, almost luxurious shopping in the same store that was selling her cough mixture and toilet soap!

Not easy! Most women much preferred the beauty-orientated reputations and fashion-driven store environments of department stores like John Lewis, Debenhams etc. We recognised that unless we changed the experience quite radically for our shoppers then we would not get their business – it was not a question of sexy new advertising – our core offer had to change.

Our first step was to re-lay as many stores as we could to separate the Beauty areas from toiletries and healthcare. In two-storey buildings we would often take Healthcare upstairs, leaving Beauty free to create an upmarket 'beauty hall' on the ground floor. This worked for both product categories – healthcare customers also had their dedicated area. The key, though, was to try to create a distinct 'Beauty area' in all stores with a different, more upmarket, more indulgent feel than the rest of the store.

Secondly, we tried to expand the space available to our Beauty product ranges – not to get more products on shelf necessarily, but to provide more display space for the premium products that we stocked. Many of these products were not cheap – to sell them they needed display space to showcase them to best effect and to create a thoughtful, indulgent shopping environment that connected with the emotions our customers felt when they were shopping for beauty products.

Finally, we upgraded the premium feel of our Beauty areas by introducing third-party brands like Ruby and Millie, Benefit and others. Each of these brands brought their own premium look and feel, plus a range of unique products that other health and beauty retailers did not have. This approach extended beyond Beauty into our Toiletries ranges too where premium brands like Soap and Glory started to bring a much more interesting and upmarket feel.

It was not that any one of these changes made the crucial difference. Rather, their combination created an environment which gave our consumers emotional 'permission' to enjoy an indulgent Beauty shopping experience. It just 'felt' different from other retailers and, without them ever making a conscious decision, we started to find consumers spending more and more of their Beauty shopping time in our stores.

For me this is a classic example of how the emotions drive shopping decisions. Consumers would never admit it – but how they 'feel' about a store makes all the difference.

It certainly worked for us!'

The Growth Director's Summary

- Don't forget: most marketing campaigns do not deliver the growth results that they were designed for.
- The single task that should be the goal for every marketer is to bring his/her brand's Catnip Proposition to its target customers impactfully and persuasively.
- Successful marketing communications for a Catnip Proposition must have two essential elements:

  - it must establish an emotional connection with your target consumers so as to secure their permission to sell; and
  - it must present a differentiating performance promise that will be meaningfully preferred at the emotionally important moments when autopilot decisions are made.

- Permission to sell is needed because our brains hardwire us to ignore or reject most marketing communications. Often, a competitive brand's advertising will generate 'an automatic and non-conscious counter-persuasion reaction' in its target customers.

- The key to securing permission to sell is to connect emotionally with target customers by showing you understand/empathise with their view of the category and its emotional goal drivers. Lynx and Dove's Campaign for Real Beauty are great examples of brands who did this successfully.
- To secure permission to sell for your brand you need to do three things:

  - understand the emotional goal territory driving purchases of your target customers in your chosen category;
  - identify the Moments of Maximum Emotional Impact when the emotions involved are at their most intense and when autopilot decisions are made; and
  - ensure your marketing and advertising campaigns evoke and connect with these emotions so that your target consumers will be emotionally open to you and ready to listen to the more rational aspects of your proposition

- Once permission to sell is secured you need to present a differentiating performance promise that persuades consumers of the superiority of your Catnip Proposition.
- Key elements of an effective differentiating performance promise are the performance elements that matter at the key Moments of Maximum Emotional Impact when autopilot decisions are made – you MUST focus on these.
- Marketing communications are most effective when they are either i) delivered at the Moments of Maximum Emotional Impact themselves (for example with financial services or Christmas gifting) or ii) are effective at evoking these MoMIs whenever they are encountered (examples are Lynx, summer holiday marketing)
- In planning media spending don't forget that the key is targeting emotional goal territories NOT socio-demographic consumer groups. Often mass media like TV/outdoor campaigns work more effectively in this regard than highly targeted campaigns driven by 'Big Data'
- Finally, never forget: 'Big Data' is often worthless unless it is guided by 'Brain Data'!

Chapter 11

So – what could possibly go wrong? An overview of all the other stuff that you can't afford to ignore

So – that all seems fairly straightforward, doesn't it?

Well in some ways, yes it is. Careful analysis of the most recent understandings of how our brains work and how we shop and make choices between brands will lead us to a blueprint of a plan to deliver significant, sustained, profitable growth – Good Growth. The outline of that plan would be:

- Identify the emotional goal territory where your brand has the best chance of becoming the default autopilot choice (your Growth Sweet Spot).
- Drill down into this territory and identify the customers or customer mind sets that account for the purchase decisions in this territory.
- Identify the Moments of Maximum Emotional Impact (MoMIs) which drive autopilot decision-making in this territory.
- Develop a Catnip Proposition to secure autopilot status for your brand which both connects emotionally with target customers at these key moments and offers a differentiating performance promise.
- Develop marketing plans which present your Catnip Proposition to target customers in a way which both secures their permission to sell and at a time when they are ready to consider making autopilot choices.

None of these things are easy to do – but, for a focused, determined Growth Director all should be very achievable. If they are delivered effectively, it is reasonable to expect that they will deliver significant, sustained, profitable growth.

So – what could go wrong?

Well, of course, the answer to that is 'plenty'. Life in the business world is not as neat and well ordered as it can appear in the pages of business books, and, even if all of the above stages are executed as well as it is possible to do, then there is still much that could prevent a business delivering the growth that it aims for.

It would be impossible to cover all the potential pitfalls that might affect a business aspiring to grow, but I will tackle three areas that are both potential problem 'hot-spots' and are also areas where risk can be mitigated to a large extent by a focused and engaged Growth Director, with a little smart preparation and planning.

These three areas are:

- Failure to address 'controlling weaknesses' in your proposition.
- Failure to notice, and act on, significant changes in competitor behaviour, consumer habits/attitudes, market/technological trends.
- Failure to keep your management team focused on the Growth Strategy.

I'll take each of these in turn.

Identifying, and addressing, 'controlling weaknesses' in your proposition

As companies focus (correctly) on developing propositions that will deliver against the most important needs at the key MoMIs it can sometimes be easy to miss, or ignore, controlling weaknesses in areas of your brand's offer that, while they may not be key to securing autopilot status and delivering growth, will prevent consumers from switching to you if they are not addressed.

Paradoxically, as a business becomes more and more focused on the critical propositional elements that will deliver autopilot status, it can be tempted to 'turn a blind eye' to other areas that are significantly weak and convince itself that it does not need to commit time and resources to addressing them.

The neuroscientific basis for this risk is quite straightforward. In any category there are two types of goals that we are trying to meet when we purchase products: explicit goals and implicit goals. The explicit goals are the basic purposes for which products are produced: removing dirt in the case of detergents, providing protection from body odour in the case of deodorants, providing a safe place to store our money in the case of banks. These explicit goals are the 'gateways' to the category: if a product fails to deliver against them it will not be chosen by consumers no matter how skilfully the brand is positioned and marketed. The problem with explicit goals, though, is that after a short period of time all category entrants provide broadly similar levels of performance and differentiation becomes very difficult.

Hence the power of the implicit emotional goals – autonomy, adventure, security, discipline, enjoyment and excitement – to provide the powerful emotional basis for differentiation and brand choice.

The risk is that in (correctly) focusing on the implicit goals to achieve differentiation and autopilot status, brands sometimes lose focus on delivering acceptably on the explicit goals, and fall below an acceptable level of performance.

Three examples from my own experience illustrate this risk very well.

Boots is too expensive!

Perhaps the most commonly ignored controlling weakness is in pricing. Many businesses who believe they offer clear superiority in areas such as product performance, service, product range, or brand image convince themselves that it is okay to be a little more expensive than their competitors. Often, it is – a little more. The risk, though, is that 'a little more' keeps getting ratcheted up by the demands of the bottom line until what had started as an acceptable premium for superior quality becomes an insurmountable barrier to autopilot choice.

Remember, in every purchase decision we make we are making a calculation to give away something we value highly – money – in order to get something else we desire – the performance the product or service is delivering. Our subconscious makes this 'cost–benefit' calculation every time we make a purchase decision. If the performance superiority that your product/service is providing stays constant (as is usually the case) but the price you are charging for it edges up over time, then at some point the 'cost–benefit' calculation tilts against you, and your customers' subconscious brains will say 'no deal'!

I encountered the affect of this common controlling weakness when I joined Boots in the mid-2000s. The team at the time believed, correctly to some degree, that their superior ranges of health and beauty products, the service provided by well trained staff, and the trusted Boots brand, justified them selling at a premium compared to the supermarket chains like Tesco who were, at the time, the key competitors.

Once this seductive logic had been accepted internally, however, it was very hard to stop prices rising inexorably year after year: the short-term (positive) impact on the bottom line of higher prices was immediate and significant, and the longer-term (negative) effect on sales trends and brand image was hard to detect. In Boots' case this trend was worsened by its tradition of running high-profile 'Buy One Get Second Half Price' (or similar) promotions across most of its ranges – this helped the management team to feel more comfortable with moving shelf prices up, hoping consumers would not notice – they did!

When I joined the business and asked to see pricing comparisons on baskets of the most popular products I was shocked to discover that a Boots basket of the most commonly purchased products from across the store was 17% more expensive than buying the same products in Tesco – 17%!

While as a newcomer it was easy for me to see what a problem this was, for the team inside the business it did not appear to be such a big issue. The Boots internal culture had got so used to the idea of selling at a premium, and had become so dependent on the margin impact these high prices provided that it was most reluctant to accept that perceived, and actual value had become a controlling weakness. Moving comparable pricing back to within the 0%-+5% range that we had identified as acceptable took around three years and was enormously hard to achieve without negatively impacting profits.

To their huge credit, the Boots buying teams managed to deliver this and, as they did so, suddenly opened the (improved) health and beauty proposition up to consumers who had been previously excluded because Boots was just too expensive. Sales trends turned around and the business embarked on a number of years of sustained, profitable growth.

Ecover doesn't clean!

More recently I have done some consultancy work with Ecover, the 'green' cleaning product company.

Ecover is very clear about its Catnip Proposition: it provides products which will clean your house and your clothes without the risk of damage to the environment caused by conventional detergents. The Ecover business is full of very smart, very driven people who are admirably committed to finding 'green' solutions and who are reluctant to compromise on these challenging principles. Over the years, Ecover has developed ranges of products that have reduced potential environmental damage to levels that would once have seemed impossible to imagine. Some of this is truly great work.

When I first began working with Ecover, however, I noticed there was one important problem that was holding the business back and which no-one seemed to care much about – the products did not clean very well!

As with the Boots example, it was not that the business was unaware of this fact – it was just that it had convinced itself that, because its Catnip Proposition was all about protecting the environment, its consumers would accept an inferior cleaning performance.

And, to an extent, some of them would, trading efficacy for 'doing the right thing' for the planet. But over time, as the gap between Ecover's performance and that of conventional cleaners became greater, and the challenge involved in addressing this became tougher and potentially more expensive, the management team became used to ignoring this discrepancy and to persuading themselves it was relatively unimportant.

Again, the task of persuading an incumbent management team to see this as a problem and to address it was difficult. To their huge credit, once they had been persuaded that unless they provided broadly comparable levels of performance to conventional cleaners then consumers would not switch to Ecover the team took on this challenge. Remarkably, they found ways to upgrade cleaning performance significantly (up to a 50% improvement in cleaning performance) without any negative effect on Ecover's environmental impact.

Result: suddenly, the group of consumers for whom Ecover was a potential autopilot choice was massively enlarged.

Mums can't go to Iceland often enough!

My third example of controlling weaknesses holding a potentially strong business back is taken from my time as marketing director at Iceland Frozen Foods in the mid/late 1990s.

Again, Iceland's Catnip Proposition was pretty clear – strong ranges of frozen food sold at low prices to middle-/low-income mums. For many years this formula had delivered strong and consistent growth, but these trends slowed in the early/mid-1990s as the supermarket chains (in particular Asda and Tesco) expanded their ranges of frozen food and matched Iceland's low prices. The supermarkets also had one built-in advantage: while mums tended to visit Iceland on foot during the week, they would use the car to do a big food shop at the weekends. Simply, this meant that they could stock up at Asda with lots of frozen food that they could then transport home by car. More Asda food in the freezer meant less space for Iceland food during the week – meant less growth for the business.

Again it took the management team some time to recognise that the controlling weakness that had developed was not down to product quality, or range, or pricing – all the traditional levers that retailers pull when sales go flat – but rather, simply, to a physical inability to carry more than one or two Iceland shopping bags home on foot.

The solution we arrived at was to launch the UK's first national home delivery food service: the results were instant and quite spectacular. For shoppers who used the home delivery service average basket spend moved from around £7.25 to over £40 – obviously a phenomenal increase. While of course not all shoppers chose to use the service, it added about 4% to the like-for-like sales of every store in which it was offered.

Again, this is transformational impact on growth by identification and addressing a controlling weakness that had previously been missed or ignored because it was not central to the company's core proposition. In each case, the importance of these weaknesses could only be understood by talking to consumers – both current and former brand loyalists – and being prepared to listen carefully to the criticisms they had, as well as to the things they liked about our business.

It's not rocket science – but if your business appears to have a strong and differentiating core proposition . . . and yet is not growing much – go and check with your consumers – chances are there's a controlling weakness in there somewhere holding you back!

Failure to notice, and act on, significant changes in competitor behaviour, consumer habits/attitudes, market/ technological trends

The second 'thing that could go wrong' is probably the most common 'banana skin' for businesses that appear to be growing nicely.

It is human nature that, when things are going well for us, we tend to assume they will continue that way far into the future. In a business context we become convinced that our proposition will continue to beat all others, that competitors who try to do things differently are making a big mistake, and that radical new technologies will be niche ideas rather than game-changers.

This tendency is (of course) rooted in the neuroscience of how our brains work. It is very well-known in the world of neuroscience and behavioural economics that we have a developed tendency to value what we have more highly than something that we might gain. Most 'loss aversion' studies show that people place about twice the value on an item they are being asked to give up compared to what they would be prepared to pay for the same item if they did not already have it.

Similarly, many studies show how we value certainty of outcome over uncertainty even if it is likely that the uncertain outcome will benefit us. So – in the telecoms industry it is well known that many (often, most) of the customers on flat-rate tariffs would be better off if they switched to variable rates. But, even when this is pointed out, most still prefer the certainty of knowing what they will be charged each month.

These built-in biases towards the status quo affect management teams too and are very dangerous to businesses. They lead us, as managers, to over-estimate the likely longevity of the propositions and strategies we are currently employing, and cause us to underrate the likely impact of new brands, new technologies, new trends. This frequently causes once-successful companies to struggle as they underestimate changes that challenge their previously successful models in new ways.

Apple has repeatedly heard its innovative new products written off at launch as 'niche' and unlikely to have mass-market appeal.

- The iPhone: 'Gimmicky – who wants to play games on a hand-set?'
- The iPad: 'Can't decide if it's a phone or a lap-top and ends up being neither.'
- Even the Macbook Air: 'Loses essential functionality by prioritising design over operation.'

Technological or design innovations like these are at least obvious and are hard to miss (particularly when they are Apple branded!). But other changes in less obvious areas like shifts in societal attitudes are harder to spot and are therefore even more likely to be ignored by incumbent management teams with seemingly successful business models.

A recent example of changing societal attitudes undermining hugely successful businesses is in the UK supermarket sector where once dominant brands like Tesco, Asda and Morrisons have fallen from grace as significant chunks of their business have switched to a new type of shop – the European-style 'hard discounter' format led by Aldi and Lidl.

These formats were launched in the UK in the early noughties, and initially had only limited success. This has changed over the last seven or eight years, though, as their share of the UK grocery market has grown significantly at the expense of the incumbent 'value based' supermarket brands. Take a look at how brand shares have changed in 2016 vs 2015 – huge growth for the new formats at the expense of the previously dominant Tesco, Asda and Morrisons.

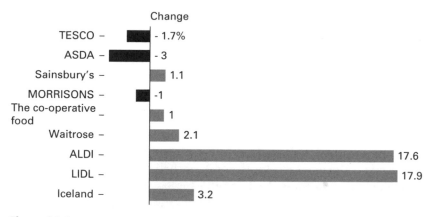

Figure 11.1

Why the surge? And why didn't the big guys spot it?

The answer lies in a shift in societal attitudes to shopping for value that the management teams at the big supermarkets either failed to pick up, or decided was not significant enough to warrant a serious response. Prior to the financial crash of 2007/2008 and subsequent recession, shoppers were fairly predictable in their choice of supermarket. Shoppers who were primarily driven by good value but also wanted to buy some better-quality products were able to do so by choosing one of the big supermarkets and mixing and matching their value ranges and special offers with their higher quality 'Tesco Finest' (or equivalent) own-label range.

While Aldi and Lidl offered even lower prices than the supermarkets, their ranges were not wide enough to offer the higher-quality choice that consumers wanted. Also, for many consumers, there was something of a social stigma associated with shopping at such 'downmarket' retailers. While relatively upmarket supermarkets like Waitrose and Sainsbury's offered wonderful ranges of quality fresh and other food, they could not compete for low value on everyday groceries.

Hence the domination of the Tesco/Asda/Morrisons models.

After 2009's financial crash, though, this all this changed. The desire for lowest possible prices on everyday products suddenly meant that Aldi and Lidl looked more attractive than ever before. As the British public's view of their economic future took a turn for the worse, so their worry about being seen to shop at 'downmarket' supermarkets receded – their priority was increasingly to search out lower prices wherever they were to be found. This brought Aldi and Lidl onto the shopping radar of new groups of consumers who previously would not have considered them.

Further, as the recession deepened, the new phenomenon of 'dual location shopping' appeared – shoppers visiting both the lowest-priced outlets (i.e., Aldi and Lidl) for the bulk of their weekly purchases as well as making a more limited trip to the highest-quality supermarkets – Sainsbury's or Waitrose – to 'treat' themselves and their families in a more limited way.

That, suddenly, left the Tesco/Asda/Morrisons proposition somewhat high and dry. Not cheap enough for the real value seekers; not high-quality enough for a 'treat'.

These trends were accelerated by Aldi and Lidl recognising their opportunity and producing some highly effective advertising that connected emotionally with the desire of Tesco/Asda/Morrisons shoppers to 'give themselves permission' to shop at the hard discounters. The advertising presented the value they offered not as the way to get the lowest prices possible, but rather as the thing that smart, sophisticated shoppers did these days. Highly effective!

One final example of how attitudinal changes in society can, if not spotted and acted on, undermine hugely successful business models is the story of the once-mighty online business Friends Reunited.

Remember Friends Reunited? Back in the late 1990s/early noughties it was just about the most successful brand in a world full of surging digital businesses. Everyone was on it – it connected you with all your old school/university/work friends, enabled you to find out what they were all doing, triggered long-overdue reunions with people who hadn't seen each other for 20 years or more . . . and also re-ignited a fair number of teenage romances!

Friends Reunited was sold to ITV in 2005 for £120million – just six years after its launch in a back bedroom in North London. What a success story!

Scroll forward just 10 years though – and Friends Reunited has disappeared. It officially closed down on 26 February 2016 – an incredible fall from grace. How could that happen with a business so popular just a few years ago.

Well, simply . . . Facebook.

The governing assumption behind Friends Reunited was that people had a strong desire to connect with old friends. And that of course was, and is, true. But what Friends Reunited missed was that there was an even more powerful desire than connecting with and 'showing off' to all your old friends – that was connecting with and 'showing off' to your existing friends – and their friends!

Between the launch of Friends Reunited and the launch of Facebook, society's attitudes to digital/social media had shifted significantly. From a largely 'transaction-based' approach ('I go online for a specific purpose – to contact the people I went to school with') to a 'lifestyle' approach ('I share everything I do, everyday, with my online/social media contacts'). Facebook 'got' this switch – Friends Reunited did not.

By concentrating on the proposition that had been so successful for them, Friends Reunited was doomed as soon as Facebook (with broadly similar technology and functionality) came along with an approach that 'trumped' theirs. They had missed a fundamental truth that, in a world where the currency is connecting with friends, current friends always trump old friends – and by the time they had realised this and tried to adapt their proposition accordingly, Facebook had established itself and had blown away all rivals.

As these case studies illustrate, spotting these societal/attitudinal changes early enough, evaluating which are likely to be the truly challenging ones, and adapting/changing your currently successful proposition to take account of this is extremely difficult.

Again, the only way for an effective Growth Director to give his/her organisation a fighting chance of noting and reacting to changes like this is to ensure that you are better than all your competitors at understanding how consumer attitudes to your business, to your competitors and to the market are changing. The key to this, as outlined in earlier chapters, is to identify and track relentlessly the attitude and behaviours of the Market Making Customers who are the high frequency/high volume/high passion consumers at the core of every category. These consumers will be the first to notice and react to emerging trends/new products/new propositions. Tracked efficiently, they can be an incredibly effective 'canary in the coalmine' for your brand.

I also strongly advocate the use of neuroscience-based tools which track emotional attitudes as well as more rational ones – these are the true determinants of whether new ideas are likely to shift 'autopilot' preference or not. Without a sense of how emotions are shifting, you will be most unlikely to spot important emerging trends or to anticipate their impact accurately. Smart Growth Directors will find these tools and use them.

Failure to keep your management team focused on the Growth Strategy

Management teams are strange, and often rather dysfunctional beasts.

Most senior teams would say that setting the strategy for a business is one of their most important functions. Most of them would probably claim that this was something that they, personally, and their management team generally, was rather good at.

Yet most businesses find sticking to a set strategy for any meaningful length of time extremely difficult.

> What kills future growth is not the market, but your own internal complexity . . . and complexity is the silent killer of growth.
>
> Allen et al. (2014)

Why is this? Why do teams of smart, focused, well-motivated managers who fully understand the importance of strategic clarity and who want to prioritise the long-term over the short-term so often end up with multiple overlapping initiatives, flip-flopping marketing campaigns, a lack of clarity on strategic priorities, and decisions driven by short-term expediency rather than long-term strategic importance?

Well, if you can remember all the way back to Chapter 1, you may recall the answer to this: *Stuff*.

In any major business the senior management are inundated daily by Stuff. Powerful, urgent, compelling Stuff that pushes them to do something – fast.

All businesses, and all management teams, acutely feel such pressure. The ability to resist this is also undermined by the essentially competitive nature of most (if not all) management teams.

Not yours? Come on . . .

It's human nature to try to displace pressure from your work team onto others. So, if sales are looking a little flat in a typical retail organisation, the stores team will blame the buying teams for a weak set of promotions; the buying teams will blame the supply chain team for not getting the new product ranges into store quickly enough; the marketing team will blame the finance team for cutting their advertising budgets; and everyone will blame the marketing team because . . . well that's what the marketing team is there for, isn't it?

This entirely natural internal competitiveness also fuels a 'we need to do something' dynamic inside businesses, which pulls them away from sticking calmly to implementing the agreed strategy, focusing on the identified target customers, emphasising the propositional elements they know are most important – and commonly leads to complex, expensive and ineffective commercial and marketing plans – and no growth. Peter Drucker nailed it:

> There is nothing so useless as doing efficiently that which should not be done at all.

Avoiding this fate is very difficult. There are, however, some steps that wise management teams – and in particular, smart Growth Directors – can take:

- agree the growth strategy, publicise it and 'sell it' – constantly;
- focus on the growth strategy frequently at Exco;
- find growth metrics that are forward looking not backward looking; and
- demand customer data to justify any move away from the plan.

Agree the growth strategy, publicise it, 'sell it' – constantly

In some ways, agreeing a growth strategy for your business is the easy bit (provided you've read this book). The danger though, is that, following that triumphant presentation to the executive committee when your growth strategy was finally endorsed, when your colleagues mouthed 'good job' across the boardroom table and the CEO pulled you to one side afterwards for a quiet 'excellent piece of work . . . well done' pep talk, you will feel as if the task has been successfully accomplished.

It hasn't. If an understanding of the agreed growth strategy goes no further than the boardroom and the executive committee then I'm afraid you'll find it hard to keep the organisation on track for more than a couple of weeks.

The task of an effective Growth Director is to 'sell' the growth strategy to the wider organisation – and keep selling it.

The first way to do this is to write the strategy down – if you can do it get it on just one page. Make it simple, impactful and memorable. Find snappy phrases that people across the organisation will remember – don't worry about being cheesy. . .cheesy gets remembered! Make clear what the key priorities for the organisation should be in delivering it – and make this as relevant to the everyday jobs of colleagues across the organisation as possible.

There are an almost infinite number of formats for documents like this – but, however it is designed there are three core elements that must always be present and should be at the core of the document. These are:

(1) *What are you trying to achieve?* What are your growth objectives and goals? To become the biggest brand in the category in three years' time? To outgrow the market over the next five years by x%? To achieve compound annual growth of x% over the next three years? Whatever the objectives, ensure they are

 (i) specific and measurable
 (ii) stretching but achievable – they MUST beat your published budget numbers or they are not worth having
 (iii) genuinely bought into by the whole organisation.

(2) *Where will your growth come from?* Specifically you MUST be clear about which groups of consumers/consumer mind-sets/buying occasions you are going to target for growth, and what changes you need to achieve to deliver your growth goals.

For example, you might target 'increasing our share of value-driven shopping occasions amongst middle/low income mums from x% to y%'; or 'becoming the autopilot beer choice of x% of young men in social situations with people they want to impress by 2020'. Specify your target consumer/mind-set/occasions; specify the change in preference you need to achieve to reach your growth goal.

(3) *How will you get there?* What is the proposition you need to bring to market to deliver the change in preference necessary to achieve your growth goals?

Ideally, you would be able to produce a simple propositional statement that would summarise your road to growth. Something like: 'We will increase our share of value-driven shopping occasions amongst middle/low-income mums from x% to y% by reducing our average basket price vs other supermarkets by 5%, funded by x margin improvements and y cost savings, and supported by marketing that single-mindedly communicates the feel-good factor delivered by saving the family money'.

Clearly, a 'real' business' growth strategy would have a lot more granularity than the illustrative examples given here – but you get the idea.

Once you have this simple, impactful document – go sell it. An effective Growth Director will put significant time against taking the strategy to all parts of the organisation, explaining it to each of the teams from senior management to shop floor, articulating why it is right for the business, and the roles their team can play in delivering it.

Don't underestimate the power of getting around your organisation in this way – buy-in (and therefore continued focus) will be massively enhanced if people feel they have been engaged in the launch process.

And don't let up with the selling effort. A smart Growth Director will get himself/herself in front of the organisation regularly, updating on progress, describing successes and challenges, outlining next steps and re-engaging support from across the business. This is time-consuming, but absolutely essential if you are to keep a complex organisation focused and committed.

Focus on the growth strategy frequently at Exco

Seems obvious – but it is amazing how fast the strategy that everyone agreed was the way forward in January can be semi-forgotten by March. Unless, that is, the Growth Director ensures it stays top of the agenda.

Once agreed, your Exco has made an implicit commitment to focus on your strategy. Don't let them off the hook! Insist on regular Exco sessions to review progress, discuss successes and challenges, gain agreement to investments needed/support from teams across the business/necessary new initiatives. Your Growth Strategy should appear on the Exco agenda as frequently as any other subject – a smart Growth Director will monitor agendas to ensure this happens – and will insist on more 'air-time' if it is not.

Don't think this is necessary? Think again. As just one example here is a pull of the subjects covered by one major UK business at its Exco meetings over 2015 (identity withheld to prevent embarrassment . . .). The Exco held 10 meetings over the year: here are the key subjects covered:

- profit progress: 10 agenda items
- general trading update/issues and opportunities: 10
- general finance issues including cash flow forecasts, debt ratios etc: 10
- cost savings progress: 7
- potential mergers/acquisitions: 3
- people issues including annual employee survey: 5
- supply chain issues: 6
- external relations/PR issues: 4
- new product initiatives: 3
- pricing issues: 3
- risk-related issues: 2
- legal matters: 4
- three- year growth strategy: 1.

Need we say more? While this is a magnificent sample size of 1, it is, in my experience, typical of the way most companies operate.

Growth Directors – pull your weight!

Find growth metrics that are forward looking not backward looking

This is difficult – but is also really important.

Almost all the growth metrics used by businesses are backward-looking, telling you plenty about what has happened in the past (which you probably know already) but very little about what is likely to happen in the future. Sales, market share, brand attribute tracking data, competitor data – all of these tend to provide a rear-view mirror sense of what is happening with your business – and all rely on rational, conscious, System 2 responses: hopefully this book has made clear why these should be treated with extreme caution.

All of these have some value but, used in isolation, are dangerous. Why? Simply because of our natural tendency to want to respond to the data we are presented with. So – if last month's sales were down we will want to respond to whatever last month's problems were. Even if these problems were short-term in nature and unrelated to the fundamental strength or otherwise of your business; even if they are described in purely rational System 2 terms that you know does not tell the whole story; even if the short-term fixes they imply are pushing you away from your long-term strategy – still you will find it very hard to resist the calls to 'do something' – fast!

The challenge for Growth Directors is to find additional metrics that measure the propensity of your brand to grow in the future. Such metrics are beginning to emerge from the world of neuroscience but are not yet in widespread use.

Essentially, you need measures of whether you have a Catnip Proposition in place that is likely to deliver autopilot preference at the Moment of Maximum Emotional Impact. This means being able to track emotional, subconscious, System 1 attitudes to your brand as well as all the traditional rational, conscious, System 2 metrics that businesses are used to.

These measures do exist. Smart Growth Directors need to connect with the companies who are able to provide them and then work to persuade their management teams that they are more reliable indicators of likely future growth than the rational, backward-looking, System 2 measures that have been common practice until now.

Don't be afraid to challenge these traditional metrics. After all:

- Even in the best of times our analysis shows that 9 out of 10 management teams fail to grow their companies profitably.

  Bain et al. (2012)

And you can be sure that nine out of 10 were all using traditional business tracking metrics...

Demand customer data to justify any move away from the plan

Finally – given that you will inevitably face pressure to focus away from your growth strategy at some point, a wise Growth Director would do well to set the bar high if changes are to be made.

Ensure that you have reinforced, again and again, the value of resisting the urge to do 'stuff' and sticking to the strategy that you have agreed as an Exco will deliver growth. But, when challenges come, try to agree that these will be evaluated properly, against the customer criteria that you have established most drive autopilot preference in your areas of business.

Again, this requires tools which can measure reaction of the subconscious, emotional, System 1 brains of your target customers – but these do exist and can be used as swiftly and cost-effectively as conventional research.

An Exco which has fully bought in to the growth strategy will understand the justification for this type of data and is more likely to be persuaded away from 'knee-jerk' responses to short-term issues if these metrics are available to them. Make these metrics as much a part of the daily basis for Exco interaction as profit margins, or revenue sales, or annualised cost savings. Ultimately, all your business – and all your profit – comes from your customers – surely decisions should be guided by their views more than anything else.

So – a brief overview of the issues that all Growth Directors are likely to face in implementing and maintaining focus against a powerful growth strategy.

These issues are not exhaustive – many others will exist. But the key mitigating activities outlined here:

- agree the growth strategy, publicise it and 'sell it' – constantly;
- focus on the growth strategy frequently at Exco;
- find growth metrics that are forward looking not backward looking; and
- demand customer data to justify any move away from the plan.

This will make a difference and will give every Growth Director a better chance of success – no matter how much 'Stuff' is thrown at them!

That, then, brings us on to the final chapter in this book – a summary of all we have learned.

The Growth Director's Summary

- The three key risks to an effective Growth Strategy are:

  - Failure to address controlling weaknesses in your proposition.
  - Failure to notice significant changes in competitor behaviour, consumer habits/attitudes, market/technological trends.
  - Failure to keep your management team focused on the Growth Strategy.

- Controlling weaknesses are usually linked to weaknesses in the basic explicit goals of the category – do not lose sight of these as you strive for a proposition differentiated at a higher emotional level
- To ensure you are on top of emerging changes you need to stay connected to your 'Market Making Customers' – the high frequency/ high volume consumers who will be at the forefront of emerging trends. Ideally this connection should include neuroscience-based tools to track emotional changes as well as functional ones
- To keep your management team focused on the Growth Strategy you need to:

  - Agree the strategy formally, publicise it and 're-sell' it frequently.
  - Force regular review of your Growth Strategy onto your Exco agenda – if your top team are not focusing on it the rest of the organisation will lose focus.

- Find growth metrics that are forward looking, measuring your readiness for future growth rather than merely recording past performance. This means tracking emotional trends as well as functional performance.
- Demand customer data to justify any move away from your agreed strategy.

Chapter 12

Summary – and The Growth Director's Secret: The Secret revealed – and what you need to do about it

So what IS 'The Growth Director's Secret'?

After all, this book has looked at the challenge of delivering significant, sustained, profitable growth from many different angles, and has uncovered a number of important insights that might be regarded as 'growth secrets' in their own way. Insights like:

- *The Growth Paradox*: the fact that, while all companies would agree that delivering growth is of great importance to them, most of them are very bad at achieving this.
- *Most companies don't take growth seriously*: by which I mean they lack clear executive accountability for growth (nobody has a 'Growth Director'); usually fail to develop clear, simple growth strategies; rarely prioritise growth as a subject in Exco discussions; and lack reliable metrics to measure current and forecast future growth performance.
- *The Big Growth Mistake* that most companies make – the assumption that all consumers, and all purchase occasions are 'up for grabs' and that the way to grow is to construct super-busy, always-on commercial plans that snatch as many of those purchases as possible. Wrong.
- *Autopilot shopping*: most of the time, to cope with the complexity of our lives, we shop on autopilot from a small portfolio of favourite brands. These autopilot brands have been chosen subconsciously, we bond emotionally with them and are very reluctant to change, and in most categories they get 75–90% of our purchases. The key to growth is becoming the default autopilot brand in your category – that's it.
- *MoMIs*: these Moments of Maximum Emotional Impact are when autopilot decisions are taken. The key to securing autopilot status is to connect with the emotions behind these moments and to offer a

proposition that will out-perform all others at these emotionally important times. Examples of brands that do this brilliantly are Lynx (moment where young man meets attractive young girl) and Premier Inn (moment of waking up refreshed and energised).

- *Target emotional goal territories, not consumers*: the classic targeting mistake is to focus on specific socio-demographic consumer types. This implicitly assumes that consumers have consistent and predictable needs and preferences. We don't. These change according to circumstances/moods/situations and so targeting at fixed socio-deomgraphic groups will inevitably lead to wastage and inefficiency. The key is to target emotional goal territories, not consumer types – the Dove 'Campaign For Real Beauty' is a classic example of a brand understanding this.

- *Market-Making Customers* – the key to understanding your category. Market-Making Customers are that high-frequency, high-volume group of customers that account for a disproportionate share of category volume, but more importantly whose attitudes, preferences and opinions set the standards for all other brands. Market-Making Customers are passionate about the category, highly opinionated and can be incredible advocates – or powerful brand wreckers. Go to school on them – it's the fastest way to understand what your brand needs to do to grow.

All great insights – and all could qualify as 'growth secrets' to some extent.

But none of these are The Growth Director's Secret. So here it is. Here's the shocking secret that needs to be addressed if businesses are to become much more effective at positioning themselves to achieve significant, sustained, profitable growth:

'Conventional research doesn't work'

That's the secret that The Growth Director wants you all to know.

Sorry – but there it is. Shocking, I know, since we have all spent huge amounts of money on focus groups, consumer surveys, depth interviews, consumer panels etc. While all these techniques are perfectly adequate for uncovering WHAT consumers do, they are almost completely ineffective at understanding WHY they do them. And unless you understand 'why' then you are most unlikely to be able to position your brand to grow.

Is it really such a big surprise? Don't we all suspect, deep down, that the research tools we've all been depending on are a bit flawed?

After all, how many of us have spent time arguing with colleagues on rival interpretations of focus groups opinions? 'Rival interpretations'? Doesn't sound like a very robust way to make a decision!

How many of us have worried when a study to choose between two alternative pack designs, or two alternative advertising ideas comes back with completely inconclusive results: 'on the one hand this pack is liked for its on-shelf impact and the perceived strength it portrays . . . but on the other hand some consumers see it as a little too harsh and masculine . . .'?

How many of us have pored over tracking data and wondered whether a decline in a rating for 'a brand for people like me' is more important than a parallel decline in the rating for 'provides high quality service' . . . and whether anyone would ever be able to tell us which we should pay more attention to?

How many of us have wondered why it is, if our research tools are so good, that around 80% of new product initiatives – surely the most-extensively researched projects we ever work on – fail to deliver their launch objectives?

I think, perhaps, we all secretly suspected that when it comes to understanding the motivations behind consumer decision-making – *conventional research just doesn't work.*

This book has spent some time explaining why this is and how our brains work in the context of shopping, purchase decision-making and brand choice. Here's a brief reprise:

Simply, our conscious System 2 brains (what we regard as us 'thinking') are slow, effortful and can only handle limited amounts of data at a time. We only use our System 2 brains for around 5–10% of all the decisions we ever make.

Most of the decisions we make are made by our subconscious System 1 brains. System 1 is intuitive, super-fast, effortless (we are rarely aware of it) and can handle huge amounts of data. Because of this super-efficiency we use System 1 for 90–95% of all the decisions we ever make – including the vast majority of our shopping decisions.

Unfortunately, conventional research interacts almost exclusively with our conscious System 2 brains. It asks rational questions and our conscious, rational, System 2 brains think carefully and provide thoughtful, rational responses. Unfortunately, since most decisions are made subconsciously by our System 1 brains, and since System 1 decisions are often driven more by emotional motivations than rational analysis, these responses are very often inaccurate and can often be downright misleading.

Without tools which can connect with the subconscious decision-making processes of our System 1 brains we are simply unable to reliably understand the motivations for the decisions we make – including the vast majority of our shopping decisions. Conventional research does not provide these. And, without this understanding of the motivational drivers behind purchase decisions and brand choice it is an almost impossible task to accurately reposition a brand to secure the default autopilot status that is the key to growth.

Now – sometimes you might get lucky. Sometimes a consumer in a focus group might make a comment that reveals the key emotional motivation behind choice of brand X or rejection of brand Y. Sometimes a particularly intuitive researcher might be able to interpret data in a way that reveals the Moments of Maximum Emotional Impact driving choice in a product category. But conventional research can offer no guarantees of this – by their very nature conventional research tools are designed to interact with our System 2 brains – and all the decisions are taken by System 1.

So – The Growth Director is very clear on this. In order to become able to position your brand or your business for significant, sustainable, profitable growth, you must find research tools that can connect with the subconscious decision-making processes of our System 2 brains. Conventional research techniques will not provide these.

Such tools have emerged, however, in the last 10 years from the world of neuroscience and are increasingly available – but far too few businesses are using them effectively. In the opinion of The Growth Director, unless repositioning work utilises the insights that these tools can provide it is most unlikely to be effective.

And this is the secret that the Growth Director wants the business world to become aware of. The insights, the behavioural models, the strategic tools that this book proposes can all only be activated effectively by businesses which are deriving their consumer insights from the subconscious decision-making processes that drive the vast majority of the decisions we ever make. That means finding and using tools that are able to connect with our System 1 brains.

For many businesses that's a difficult challenge. Most of the western business world has depended upon conventional research tools – focus groups, tracking studies, consumer surveys, consumer panels etc – for 50 years or more. Accepting that these tools are not able to provide the full range of necessary insights will be tough for many businesses – but is essential if they want to grow.

The Growth Director predicts that, in exactly the same way that the business world went from a standing start to fully digitally enabled over about a 10-year period around the turn of the century, 10 years from now use of these neuroscience-based tools will be the norm.

- Conventional research will be used solely to answer the 'what?' questions – leaving neuroscience-based tools to handle the far more important 'why?'
- Focus Groups will never again be used to answer questions about consumer motivations. No more 'Which pack design do you prefer – and why?'; no more 'How does that ad make you feel?' These questions will be answered by quantitative tools that connect with the subconscious, emotional part of our brains where these decisions are made and will give us definitive validated answers to these key questions.
- Media planners will target Emotional Goal Territories rather than consumer socio-demographics. No more expecting us to behave like robotic automatons, never deviating from a set of brand choices no matter how our circumstances change.

- Tracking studies will no longer record meaningless information such as how well consumers say they 'like' you or feel 'you are a brand for people like me' – but will monitor the connection of brands to the emotional motivations driving purchase decisions in any given category – and will record straight-line correlations between scores on these metrics and growth performance.
- Emotional insights will be data-based and validated rather than depending on the advertising agency's intuition (or, even worse, the views of the chairman's golf buddy).

In essence – the business world will increasingly recognise that an understanding of the subconscious motivations that drive everything we do has to be at the heart of all successful business strategies, and that neuroscience-based tools must be deployed in order to facilitate this.

Those companies that come to understand this first will be the ones who are the growth superstars of the next decade.

Simply put – Brain Data trumps Big Data – every time.

And that's the Growth Director's Secret.

List of references

Chapter 1

Allen, James, Bain and Company (2014) *The 5 Pillars of Sustainable Growth*. Available online at: www.bain.com/publications/articles/five-pillars-of-sustainable-growth-audio-slideshow.aspx (accessed 20/8/15).

Atsmon, Yuval and Smit, Sven (2015) Why Its Still a World of Grow or Go, *McKinsey Quarterly* October 2015.

Buzzell, Robert D, Gale, Bradley T. and Sultan, Ralph G.M. (1975) *Market Share: A Key to Profitability*. Boston: Harvard Business Press.

Hammer, Michael and Champy, James (1993) *Reengineering the Corporation*. New York: Harper Business.

McKinsey Quarterly (2007) Survey of 100 top US companies. Available online at: www.mckinsey.com/quarterly/overview (accessed 20/8/15).

McKinsey Quarterly (2008): Survey of 200 global companies. Available online at: www.mckinsey.com/quarterly/overview (accessed 20/8/15).

Zook, Chris (2001) *Profit from the Core*. Boston: Harvard Business Press.

Chapter 2

Blocki, Richard (2015) *How to Build Enduring Campaigns*. Available online at: www.linkedin.com/in/richard-blocki (accessed 24/8/15).

McKinsey Global Innovation Survey (2015) McKinsey Quarterly. Available online at: www.mckinsey.com/.../innovation-and-commercialization-2010-mckinsey-global-survey. (accessed 20/8/15).

Ries, Al and Trout, Jack (1981) *Positioning: The Battle for Your Mind*. New York: McGraw Hill.

Sharp, Byron (2010) *How Brands Grow*. Melbourne: Oxford University Press Australia.

Swalek, Joe (2013) *How Longevity Can Bring Success to Marketing Campaigns*. Available online at: www.fi.deluxe.com (accessed 24/8/15).

Chapter 3

Barden, Phil (2013) *Decoded*. Chichester: John Wiley & Sons Ltd.

Guardian Media Section, Monday 20 November 2000. Available online at www.theguardian.com.

Kahneman, Daniel (2011) *Thinking Fast and Slow*. New York: Penguin.
Sharp, Byron (2010) *How Brands Grow*. Melbourne: Oxford University Press Australia.

Chapter 4

Barden, Phil (2013) *Decoded*. Chichester: John Wiley & Sons Ltd.
Genco, Stephen J., Pohlmann, Andrew P. and Steidl, Peter (2013) *Neuromarketing for Dummies*. Mississauga: John Wiley & Sons Canada.
Kahneman, Daniel (2011) *Thinking Fast and Slow*. New York: Penguin.
Nisbett, Richard E. and Wilson, Timothy D. (1977) *Telling More Than We Can Know: Verbal Reports on Mental Processes*. *Psychological Review* (by the American Psychological Association) vol. 84, no. 3. Available online at: www.people. virginia.edu (accessed 20/10/15).

Chapter 6

Genco, Stephen J., Pohlmann, Andrew P. and Steidl, Peter (2013) *Neuromarketing for Dummies*. Mississauga: John Wiley & Sons Canada.

Chapter 7

Barden, Phil (2013) *Decoded*. Chichester: John Wiley & Sons Ltd.

Chapter 9

Allen, James, Bain and Company (2014) *The 5 Pillars of Sustainable Growth*. Available online at: www.bain.com/publications/articles/five-pillars-of-sustainable-growth-audio-slideshow.aspx (accessed 20/8/15).
Barden, Phil (2013) *Decoded*. Chichester: John Wiley & Sons Ltd.
Blackburn, Inez (2008) *Speed to Market: Capitalizing on Demands*. Available online at www.markettechniques.com.
Christensen, Clayton (2009), TechPoint Innovation Summit. Available online at: www.youtube.com/watch?v=s9nbTB33hbg (accessed 5/12/15).
Meyer-Waarden, Lars and Benanvent, Christophe (2010) *The Impact of Loyalty Programmes on Repeat Purchase Behaviour*. Available online at: www.anzmac. org/conference_archive/2003/papers/MO21_meyer-waardenl.pdf (accessed 5/12/15).

Sharp, Byron (2010) *How Brands Grow*. Melbourne: Oxford University Press Australia.

Chapter 10

Genco, Stephen J., Pohlmann, Andrew P. and Steidl, Peter (2013) *Neuromarketing for Dummies*. Mississauga: John Wiley & Sons Canada.
Riebe, Erica (2003) *How To Grow A Brand: Retain or Acquire Customers?* Available online at: https://ore.exeter.ac.uk/repository/bitstream/handle/10871/16792/Aqudef.pdf (accessed 10/12/15).
Sharp, Byron (2010) *How Brands Grow*. Melbourne: Oxford University Press Australia.

Chapter 11

Allen, James, Bain and Company (2014) *The 5 Pillars of Sustainable Growth*. Available online at: www.bain.com/publications/articles/five-pillars-of-sustainable-growth-audio-slideshow.aspx (accessed 20/8/15).
Bain and Company Insights (2012) *The Strategic Principles of Repeatability*. Available online at www.bain.co.
Drucker, Peter: multiple online sources. Available at: www.goodreads.com/author/quotes/12008.Peter_F_Drucker (accessed 15/12/15).

Index

Italic page numbers are used for figures, **bold** is used for shaded box text.